# Students Who Drive You Crazy

## Succeeding With Resistant, Unmotivated, and Otherwise Difficult Young People

### Jeffrey A. Kottler

**CORWIN PRESS, INC.**
A Sage Publications Company
Thousand Oaks, California

*For information:*

Corwin Press
A Sage Publications Company
2455 Teller Road
Thousand Oaks, California 91320
www.corwinpress.com

Sage Publications Ltd.
1 Oliver's Yard
55 City Road
London EC1Y 1SP
United Kingdom

Sage Publications India Pvt. Ltd.
B-42, Panchsheel Enclave
Post Box 4109
New Delhi 110-017  India

Printed in the United States of America

**Library of Congress Cataloging-in-Publication Data**

Kottler, Jeffrey A.
    Students who drive you crazy: Succeeding with resistant,
unmotivated, and otherwise difficult young people / by Jeffrey A. Kottler.
        p. cm.
    Includes bibliographical references and index.
    ISBN 0-7619-7875-5 (c) — ISBN 0-7619-7876-3 (p)
    1. Problem children—Education.  I. Title.
LC4801 .K65 2002
371.93—dc21
                                        2001004493

This book is printed on acid-free paper.

06  07   7   6   5   4   3

Acquisitions Editor:        Rachel Livsey
Editorial Assistant:        Phyllis Cappello
Production Editor:          Olivia Weber
Typesetter/Designer:        Denyse Dunn
Indexer:                    Teri Greenberg
Cover Designer:             Tracy E. Miller
Production Artist:          Michael Dubowe
Copy Editor:                Rachel Hile Bassett

# Contents

Preface                                                              vii

About the Author                                                      xii

1.  **Why Do Some Students Drive You Crazy?**                          1
    At a Loss About What to Do                                         2
    In the Eye of the Beholder                                         4
    So, Who Gets to You?                                               6

2.  **Which Students Challenge You Most?**                            7
    Students From Hell                                                 8
    Questions to Ask Yourself                                         23

3.  **Understanding Students' Challenging Behavior**                  26
    They Are Doing the Best They Can                                  26
    Additional Functions of Conflict                                  32
    When Biology Has Its Say                                          35
    Creating Difficult Students                                       35
    Multiple Viewpoints                                               37

4.  **What They Do to Make You Crazy**                               39
    Separating Students and Behavior                                  40
    Those Who Don't "Fight Fair"                                      41
    Protecting Yourself                                               42
    Pushing Our Buttons                                               44
    How Failure Helps                                                 48
    Engaging the Challenging Student                                  51
    How Can You Help Yourself?                                        52
    Don't Take the Conflict Personally                                53
    It Comes With the Territory                                       54

5. **Changing Your Own Behavior**     **56**
   Detachment Without Withdrawal     56
   Talking to Yourself     57
   Processing Disappointments Internally     59
   Stop Complaining     61
   Keeping Your Sense of Humor     62
   Reframing Problems     62
   Being Flexible     63
   Help Yourself First     65

6. **Strategies for Changing Students' Behavior**     **66**
   Some Rules of Engagement     66
   Strategic Interventions     77
   Resolving Conflicts     82

7. **Parents and Colleagues Who Drive You Crazy**     **86**
   The Least of Our Problems     87
   Teachers Who Don't Understand     87
   Administrators Who Handcuff Us     89
   Parents Who Fight Us     89
   Strategic Interventions     92
   What About You?     94
   Those Who Abuse You     97

8. **Preventing Future Problems**     **100**
   Proactive Versus Reactive Strategies     101
   Paying Attention to Feedback     103
   Teacher Strategies That Maintain Momentum     105
   Conflict Resolution     108
   In Summary     112

**References and Suggested Readings**     **113**

**Index**     **119**

# Preface

T he title of this book may sound flippant and irreverent, but it is actually quite carefully constructed. Rather than being a book about difficult students, this is more a study of the challenging interactions that take place between students who *appear* difficult and their teachers, counselors, and school administrators. In other words, this is a book about *you* as much as it is about *them*.

## Who This Book Is For

This book, written for elementary and secondary teachers, as well as for counselors, administrators, and other school personnel, addresses the challenges of remaining vibrant, excited, and enthusiastic about one's work when faced with some students who seem to drive you crazy. They get under your skin, haunt your dreams, and invade your consciousness at the most inopportune moments. They appear uncooperative and resistant, sometimes downright hostile and dangerous. They come in a variety of shapes and sizes, yet each of them has in common an influence on you that feels toxic and discouraging. No matter what you do or what you try with these students, you end up feeling more frustrated and ineffective.

## Unique Features

This book provides educators with a model for assessing, under-standing, and responding to their most challenging interactions at school, whether with students, parents, or colleagues. It addresses some of the most difficult problems we face today: gangs, violence, disrespect, addictions, verbal abuse, lack of motivation, and obstructiveness. It covers the kinds of conflicted relationships that occupy so much of your time and energy and that often pollute your personal life as well as your professional morale.

*Students Who Drive You Crazy* brings together most of what is known about the subject of difficult student relationships—specifically those children who appear needy, hostile, bored, unmotivated, withdrawn, isolated, inarticulate, manipulative, attention seeking, seductive, or otherwise disruptive. It draws not only on the research and literature in education but also on current practices in the related disciplines of nursing, social work, psychology, counseling, and family therapy. After all, almost every helping professional encounters more than his or her fair share of resistant people.

In addition to synthesizing the theory and research on the subject of difficult student relationships, lengthy interviews were conducted with a number of practicing teachers, counselors, and school administrators, as well as with current and "retired" students who have been known to drive teachers crazy. Their voices speak clearly about their sources of frustration as well as about what made the greatest difference in overcoming obstacles.

## Contents of the Book

In the first two chapters, we examine those students whom educators view as being their most difficult challenges. Although there is some consensus on this subject—for instance, children who are hostile, manipulative, withdrawn, or unmotivated—there are also wide differences in how such cases are defined. One of the most interesting aspects of this subject is that the students who might drive you crazy are actually those whom I might enjoy the most; likewise, the students I struggle with the most might very well be among your favorite relationships. What this means, of course, is that labels of "difficult," "resistant," or even "emotionally disturbed" are often in the eye of the beholder. One teacher really likes students who are quiet, compliant, and obedient, whereas another teacher classifies this "passivity" as most challenging to work with. Another teacher actually prefers working with students who might be described as "smart-asses," because she finds their sense of humor and energy refreshing. It will therefore be interesting for you to consider those students, parents, or colleagues with whom you have consistently encountered the most trouble. I would be willing to guess there is a pattern evident.

Chapter 3 looks at the question of why some children act so belligerently and uncooperatively. Until you can figure out what students are getting out of their behavior, and the particular context for its meaning, you won't be very successful in changing the nature of your interactions. This means examining the cultural, gender, familial, and larger systemic forces that shape and influence the way students behave. You can drive yourself crazy trying your hardest to make inroads with students when everything you try may be undone once they leave your influence. Their peer group, family values, neighborhood environment, cultural identity, and other factors are every bit as powerful as anything you can do. Unless you can understand and harness those forces, your efforts to change dysfunctional patterns will be futile.

The fourth chapter moves away from the students who drive you crazy and instead helps you examine what you do to make things difficult for yourself. Why do certain children get under your skin? What in you is getting in the way of your being more helpful? What are your own unresolved issues that interfere with your ability to be more effective? And perhaps most important of all: What can you do to help yourself when you find yourself stuck in conflicts that don't seem to have a satisfactory resolution? In much the same way that we try to help students to think through problems logically, talk to themselves more constructively, reframe things in a more positive light, and alter their perceptions of situations, you too can benefit from taking your own best advice.

Chapter 5 introduces strategies that help you to change your own internal framework when facing students who drive you crazy. The first place to begin is with your own perceptions and attitudes. If you can get yourself to the point where you are cool, calm, and collected, then almost any intervention you employ is going to be more effective.

Chapter 6 contains a fairly comprehensive catalog of things that you can do differently with your most difficult relationships. Rules of engagement are provided, as well as ways to challenge yourself to work in more flexible, creative ways. One conception of someone who is driving you crazy is that you are stuck doing the same ineffective things over and over again.

Chapter 7 deals with the thorny issue of difficult colleagues, as well as parents who drive you crazy. The same principles and strategies that have been described throughout this book can be applied as well to those situations in which you find yourself at odds with anyone else in your life. Certainly, unruly children make our lives more difficult than they need to be, but often our major sources of stress stem from other teachers, parents, and administrators who do not appreciate our work.

The final chapter concludes with a review of the major concepts that have been presented. This synthesis helps you to prevent problems that may arise in the future.

# *Acknowledgments*

I am once again grateful to Gracia Alkema, president of Corwin Press, with whom I have enjoyed a conflict-free relationship for over 25 years. After working together on over a dozen books, I am continuously amazed by her ability to combine the best qualities of the critical editor with those of the most compassionate counselor. She has been and remains one of my most important mentors.

I also wish to thank the following individuals, who reviewed the manuscript and offered many valuable suggestions:

Steve H. Hall
Technology Education Teacher
Cheatham County Central High
Ashland City, Tennessee

Fredella Stewart
Principal
Santa Teresa High School
East Side Union High School District
San Jose, California

Rick Heidt
Associate Director, Student Activities
North Dakota Council of Educational Leaders
Bismarck, North Dakota

Debra S. Preston
Psychology and Counseling
University of North Carolina at Pembroke
Pembroke, North Carolina

Gerald Monk
Associate Professor
Director of School Counseling
San Diego State University
San Diego, California

Karen Coblentz
Principal, Dassel Elementary
Dassel-Cokato School District
Dassel, Minnesota

# About the Author

**Jeffrey A. Kottler, PhD,** has worked as a teacher, counselor, and professor in a variety of settings including primary, secondary, and university levels. He is the author or coauthor of over 50 books in education and psychology, including *Beyond Blame: A New Way of Resolving Conflicts in Relationships* (1994), *The Language of Tears* (1996), *What's Really Said in the Teachers Lounge: Provocative Ideas About Cultures and Classrooms* (1997), *Secrets for Secondary School Teachers: How to Succeed in Your First Year* (1998), *Counseling Tips for Elementary School Principals* (1998), *Counseling Skills for Teachers* (2000), *On Being a Teacher* (2000), *Doing Good: Passion and Commitment for Helping Others* (2000), *Nuts and Bolts of Helping* (2000), *Making Changes Last* (2001), and *Theories in Counseling and Therapy* (2002).

Jeffrey is currently Professor and Chair of the Counseling Department at California State University, Fullerton.

# CHAPTER 1

# Why Do Some Students Drive You Crazy?

Quick. Who comes to mind when you think about your most challenging students? I am talking about those (ideally) few individuals who trouble you the most. These are the ones you think about as you drive home after work, as you drift off to sleep at night, or during idle moments when you are not otherwise occupied. Some will haunt you until the day you die.

You spend a disproportionate amount of time thinking about a few students (or parents) who drive you crazy. These are usually those who appear belligerent, uncooperative, obstructive, and resistant. Sometimes they are downright hostile or even violent.

Students drive you crazy in many ways. They challenge your authority. They question your competence and have you doing the same. They may be either so disruptive that it's hard to get much done or so withdrawn they seem impervious to anything you could do. They play mind games. Even when they do make progress, they refuse to acknowledge the gains, or at least that you had anything to do with the improvement. They frustrate you to the point that you want to scream, throttle them, or leave education altogether.

## At a Loss About What to Do

The child shows up in front of your desk holding a crumpled-up piece of paper in his fist. He looks vaguely familiar, but he is not one of your regular students. You must have seen him around school somewhere, but you can't remember the context. With a sigh, you figure this is another transfer student, and an impatient one at that: The boy is nervously tapping the chain dangling from his book bag against the side of your desk.

You are tempted to ask him to stop making the annoying sound but decide this is not the best way to begin a new relationship. You put on your best friendly face, with an inviting smile, and ask him to have a seat. He continues standing, increasing the rat-a-tat jangle of the chain.

With a visible show of patience, you ask what he is doing in your room. He flips the scrunched-up piece of pink paper in his hand onto your desk. It slides across the slick surface and lands in your lap. The boy curls his lips into a satisfied smile.

"What's so funny?" you ask him, in a voice that is a little more strident than you intended. It's been a long day, and you can immediately see that you have another challenge to deal with.

Just under his breath, you are almost positive you hear him swear at you.

"Excuse me?" you challenge him. "What was that you said?"

"Nothing," the student mumbles. He stares beyond you at the wall as if he is searching for something he lost.

"I'd like you to sit down here for a moment. I think we have some things to discuss." You pause for a moment and then add, "And could you please stop banging that chain?"

The boy looks you right in the eyes, hesitates for a moment, then shakes his head. "I don't think so."

The student then turns around and walks out of the room, leaving you to stare at the little ball of paper now resting on your desk. Not sure what else to do, you carefully unravel the referral slip that was filled out by an assistant principal. It reads: "This student seems to have a problem with authority. Please talk to him and see what you can do with him." Right.

This challenging student just happens to be of a cultural background different from your own. Interestingly, he is not like this in all of his classes or with all authority figures. In fact, with his music teacher, who is of the same ethnic background, he is one of the most cooperative and motivated students in the class. Clearly, what has transpired between you and the student, as well as between him and a few others, is not only about unacceptable and inappropriate behavior in need of control but also about cultural differences between you. There is a noteworthy absence of understanding that all of the participants in this conflict feel toward one another. Each feels very much like a victim. Furthermore, after this interaction is over, both will receive considerable sympathy from their respective peers as to how misunderstood they have been.

When you return to the staff lounge and talk about this annoying interaction, your friends will shake their heads in sympathy—for a moment anyway, until they trot out their own stories about kids who drive them crazy. When you run into the assistant principal later and he asks you how things went with the new kid, he will be very understanding about your report, because he has his own troubled history with this child. You will feel affirmed that you did nothing wrong, that in fact, none of this really had anything to do with you: This is just another instance of a troublemaker who has no interest in learning and only wants to make trouble for others.

If we would look in on the boy a little later and see him huddled in a circle with his peers, we would hear him tell a similar story of feeling disrespected and misunderstood. His perception of that interaction was that you had written him off before he opened his mouth: You didn't like him and would never give him a chance. You are just like all the other teachers he has had problems with.

This could not be further from the truth, you are quick to point out. You felt no initial animosity toward this student; you hadn't even met him yet. You were fully prepared to give him the best chance possible, to do everything in your power to help him succeed. After all, that's why the assistant principal transferred the boy to your class in the first place—because he thought you might get through to him. Well, there's no chance for that now. Or it sure seems that way.

## In the Eye of the Beholder

Although we might all agree that this student who swore at the teacher and then stormed out of the room—all without *apparent* provocation—would be a challenging case for almost anyone, such consensus is not always possible in other cases. In fact, there is remarkable diversity in the opinions of teachers, counselors, and school administrators as to what constitutes a "difficult" student.

Imagine, for example, the following scenario: You intend to present a new unit in class and decide to assess what the students already know about the subject. You ask them to take out a paper and pencil and prepare for a pretest on the lesson. One student raises her hand. You recognize her, puzzled because you see a look of determination on her face. She asks you, politely but firmly, "Why are we doing this?"

How would you interpret this student's behavior?

Of course, this is an unfair question without making other contextual cues available to you—her tone of voice, the previous patterns of her behavior, the responses of her fellow students. Nevertheless, consider your assessment of what you think this question means and how you react, viscerally, to it.

A number of possibilities are articulated by several different teachers:

Teacher A: I think she is challenging me, forcing me to be on the defensive.

Teacher B: She seems to feel a need to exert some control. Maybe she is feeling threatened. She probably didn't do her homework again that day.

Teacher C: I think she's nervous about the test and is trying to think of a way to postpone it.

Teacher D: I *like* the question. I think that is a reasonable request. If this were me, I would have provided a clearer explanation of what we were doing and why.

Teacher E: I wouldn't think anything at all. I don't have enough information to determine what she is really asking. It could mean anything.

Each of these hypotheses is perfectly reasonable. What is most interesting about so-called difficult students is that not everyone agrees who they are. If we get a group of teachers together to describe their most challenging students, we hear quite a variety of nominations:

- "For me, it's the student who is hostile, the one who has a chip on his shoulder, and it *is* usually a he."
- "I really struggle with the student who is obviously capable but doesn't apply him- or herself, doesn't study at all or turn in any work."
- "I don't like the student who always talks back and has to have the last word."
- "I can deal with anyone but the student who is withdrawn. She sleeps in the back of the room. Doesn't have any life in her."
- "I don't like students who are passive, without any opinions of their own. They are teacher-pleasers, always trying to figure out what I want to hear."
- "The student who gives me the most trouble is the one who is manipulative and plays mind games. Everything is about control."
- "I don't like students who are dishonest. I don't mind if they are surly as long as they show how they feel. I have trouble with those who pretend to feel one thing but show me a smoke screen."

Certainly these comments describe familiar characters in our classrooms. Each of us has struggled, at one time or another, with students who resemble many of these descriptions, just as each of us has encountered individuals like the defiant boy who threw the paper on the desk and walked out of the room. The point is that what constitutes a challenging student is not necessarily the same for all teachers. In many cases, it is not just the *students'* behavior that makes them difficult in the first place; it is how *we* react to what they do. In other words, students do not just come to us as challenging students. Sometimes we make them that way.

## So, Who Gets to You?

In the example that began this chapter, could another teacher have handled the situation in such a way that the boy would have been more responsive? Was it just because the teacher had white skin and a particular accent that made it impossible for the child to co-operate? Is there a way that things could have been handled differently so that this new relationship might have started on a different path? Or, more to the point, what could the teacher do now to repair what has begun as a conflicted interaction? The story is far from over, particularly because so many of our best relationships with students began in hardly the most ideal circumstances. In some situations, diversity, conflict, disagreements, and even heated exchanges can lead to very respectful, productive encounters at later times. This is particularly the case if we are able to sort out what is really going on, not just on the surface—where it seems as if a student is just being ornery—but in terms of the underlying issues that account for behavior that appears so incomprehensible.

In the next chapters, we examine some of the most important questions related to our subject: Which students challenge *you* the most, and what does this mean? How do these children get underneath your skin? Why do they act the way they do? What can you do to respond to such provocations in more effective ways? How can you apply these same strategies and skills to other conflicted relationships?

We begin with a look at the students who are most often reported as driving teachers, counselors, and administrators crazy.

# CHAPTER 2

---

# *Which Students Challenge You Most?*

I t is an enlightening exercise to begin our investigation by focusing not on the students who drive you crazy but rather on your own reactions to their behavior. As you look back at your career, or even throughout your life, who are the people who get underneath your skin most consistently? Who are the ones, over and over again, who give you the most trouble?

These are not easy questions to examine, and I must say that I am among the first to plead denial. It was my teenaged son who first pointed out to me that the same people I was constantly complaining about at work were familiar to him. "Dad," he asked me one day, although he was already certain of the answer, "isn't this guy just like that other one you used to talk about so much at your last job?" Needless to say, my son was frustrated and still a bit perturbed with me that I had uprooted our family largely to escape the abuse of a previous supervisor, only to find his spirit present once again in another body. This got me looking very closely at the patterns of people who have most consistently plagued me throughout my life, and I found that most fit a similar profile.

# Students From Hell

When I first began doing research in this area of working with difficult students, I had this great idea for a book aimed at psychologists and social workers called "Clients From Hell." At the time, I was seeing about 30 clients per week in individual therapy and had been doing so for about 10 years. It seemed to me that over the years my clients—many of them belligerent adolescents—had become more and more difficult and resistant. Like teachers, counselors, and administrators, when therapists get together we spend considerable time bitching, moaning, and complaining about how unappreciated we are and swapping "war stories" of the latest indignities we have been forced to suffer.

In that book, I visualized a chapter on each of the most notorious "clients from hell" who plagued my life. I'm sure you can nominate your own candidates for inclusion. There would be a chapter on the surly, angry student. There would be another on the person who doesn't talk, who won't say a single word no matter what you try. There would be a chapter on the violent client, the one in denial, the one who is manipulative or withdrawn or chronically depressed. Well, you get the picture.

One of the reviewers who looked at the early manuscript suggested that perhaps I might have a problem myself since I was seeing so many of my clients as difficult. Maybe I was the one with the problem, he prompted. The title of the book was immediately changed from "Clients From Hell" to "Compassionate Therapy," because I realized that I had lost my compassion for the people I was trying to help. Just like in my personal life, the same sort of person had been driving me crazy, with my students as with my clients a similar phenomenon emerged: With every group of new students I would frequently recognize the same type of individual who challenges my competence and ignites feelings of self-doubt. It turns out that I've been having trouble with the same student over and over again even though he or she takes on different forms and shapes.

## Interactive Effects

One of the reviewers for *this* book commented that the approach I was taking that emphasizes teacher perceptions was letting kids off the hook. In this professional's opinion, I was absolving them of responsibility for their own behavior and was instead perpetuating the belief that disruptive actions are never the students' fault. The reviewer thought that I might be asserting that outside forces, social causes, and so on, were the responsible parties and that personal consequences of behavior were not really the offender's responsibility.

Well, this is not at all what I mean to do. By asking you to look at your own behavior, as well as that of the students who drive you crazy, I only wish to emphasize the principle that almost all conflicts result from complex, interactive effects. Blame is not only difficult to assign accurately but not all that useful in the first place.

With this caveat, let us proceed to a review of those "students from hell" who are most often mentioned by educators. Although it is true that these kids don't really stay up late at night planning ways to make our lives miserable, it sure feels that way sometimes. In truth, they are just doing the best they can with lives that feel very much out of control.

In spite of the differences of opinion among teachers, counselors, and administrators, we can reach some consensus as to which difficult students are cited most frequently. Basically, they can be grouped into several broad categories.

## Those Who Violate Rules

Perhaps most commonly, we must confront students who, for one reason or another, decide that the boundaries that we have established do not apply to them. These rule violations can occur universally or selectively, depending on mood and context.

This situation can occur for a number of reasons:

1. Students may believe the rules are not fair or that they are not enforced consistently. There is nothing that irks young people more than the perception of favoritism or inequity. A student turns in his assignment late, then becomes indignant when it is marked down a grade. He knows someone else in the class who was granted an exception without such consequences.
2. Students might not understand what is expected. Perhaps the rules are not clearly stated, or they do not make sense in the

context of the student's culture. A new arrival from Nepal who speaks English rather well has been told to indicate by nodding her head if she understands what is being said. When she persistently shakes her head no, the teacher interprets it as defiance when, in fact, these gestures are opposite in her country.

3. Students may enjoy the benefits of not playing by the rules—the power they wield, the attention they receive, the control they feel. Natasha, for instance, knows very well that smoking is not tolerated anywhere on school property, much less in the girls' bathroom. It is almost as if she is asking to be caught, defying you and anyone else you can mobilize to stop her from doing something she is determined to do. She has not yet responded to any discipline or strategy you have used. She states clearly that you simply can't make her do anything. You are beginning to believe her.

In any situation in which you encounter rule violations, before you intervene you must first determine what the behavior means. Is this evidence of defiance, ignorance, injustice, or just plain inattention? You must also sort out the extent to which the boundary violation may be occurring because of the nature of the rules you have established and the inconsistent ways in which you are enforcing them.

Assuming that the rules are fair, reasonable, consistent, and useful, the intervention itself should be designed to help students take responsibility for the consequences of their own behavior. If they know what will happen as a result of their transgressions, then in a sense they are asking for such limit setting. Students who consistently violate rules are communicating that they lack self-control, personal responsibility, and respect for others—they are driving you (and others) crazy because they desperately need to be held within reasonable boundaries (Gootman, 2001).

## Those Who Have Given Up

Beware of anyone who feels that he or she has nothing left to lose. Some children resort to hostility, even violence, because they do not see other options. They need to exaggerate their power; they believe that the world is a very dangerous place, that others will hurt them if they see any signs of weakness, and that the best way to protect themselves is through intimidation (Roth, 1991).

Generally speaking, we like our students to be fairly articulate; to express what they are feeling in honest, sincere, and respectful ways; and to be grateful for our best intentions to help them. Children who have given up tend to be either withdrawn and nonresponsive or passionately angry and nonresponsive. In either case, they will not acknowledge our assistance, nor will they cooperate in ways that we would prefer.

Mickey doesn't talk very often, but then he does not need to say very much to communicate his utter disdain for you and everything for which you stand. He barely attends to what you are saying, apparently lost in a world of his own that you can't begin to understand. Sometimes he looks at you for a moment in pity, as if you are the one in need of help. Otherwise, he rocks in his chair, humming some tune that begins to grate on your ears. He knows that, of course, and so sings a little louder.

Another kind of student who has given up is the one who is unmotivated. Such children feel little drive to accomplish school-related tasks. In fact, they may be tremendously motivated to do other things at home, in their neighborhoods, or on school grounds, even if such behavior often goes unappreciated by adults.

Felicia, for example, appears to be a lump of clay to her teachers. She sits quietly in class, sometimes even naps, and rarely speaks to anyone. She has yet to turn in a single homework assignment; when she is asked about this noncompliance, she simply shrugs. She seems fairly bright, from what you've observed, but when called on directly in class, she rarely responds. If ever there was an unmotivated child, it is Felicia.

Away from the view of school, however, Felicia is intensely motivated to help her younger sisters. Because her parents are rarely around, the responsibility falls primarily on her to get her siblings dressed in the morning, feed them, entertain them, protect them, and get them places they need to be. Remarkably, she even helps them with their homework, even though she does not do her own. Although

Felicia appears to be unmotivated, her lack of commitment is limited mostly to school grounds, not the areas of her life she considers to be most important.

## Those Who Are Manipulative

Students often challenge us when they have a hidden agenda. You cannot take at face value what is being presented. A student comes to you with an apparently genuine request for assistance, to which you graciously respond. Then you discover that there is some other agenda at work here, one at which you can only guess. Another student is a master at "working the system." She knows exactly how to get her way, to get administrators, her parents, and other students to do her bidding. Still another manipulative student plays lots of games to keep you at a distance. There is something about you that is perceived as threatening to him, so he does everything he can think of to get you to reject him.

Nyla tells you how much you are helping her. She is so grateful for all that you have done on her behalf. You are puzzled by this: You can't remember that you have done all that much for her. You are also suspicious about her supposed changes: She looks the same to you, and her performance on work is still mediocre. When you point this out to her, she acts misunderstood and hurt. When you attempt to deal with these feelings, she takes quite another tack. The more you talk to her, the more confused you feel, unable to sort out what is real for her and what is part of her elaborate game to keep you off balance.

## Those Who Withhold Communication

This group includes students who are passive or withdrawn or who otherwise do not communicate fully, at least according to what we usually expect. This challenging student may remain silent almost all the time, speaking only when absolutely forced to do so. Even then, the student may answer in monosyllables. This is often not because the student does not have opinions or is unable to express them. The student may just be a quiet person, or he or she may be part of a culture in which speaking directly to authority figures is not considered appropriate. The student may be depressed, troubled, insecure, or lacking in confidence. The student may also have limited English skills that he or she is reluctant to admit to anyone (Kottler & Kottler, 2002).

Then there are those students who restrict the content of what they say. They may ramble a lot, intellectualize about subjects unrelated to the present discussion, or ask rhetorical questions just to hear themselves speak. The challenge with them is not that they do not contribute but that they do so in a way that precludes meaningful communication.

Another type of challenging student that fits within this category is the withdrawn student. Withdrawn students may drive us crazy precisely because nothing we do or say seems to get through to them. Ordinarily, withdrawn students do not come to your immediate attention because they don't make overt trouble and therefore often go unnoticed. Their school performance will suffer, and they will not participate in normal activities, but they don't exactly drive teachers crazy as much as concern or frustrate them.

There could be many reasons for the observed isolation:

- Lack of social skills
- Minimal English-language skills
- Recent trauma or abuse
- Chronic mistrust of authority figures
- Poor self-esteem
- Fear of intimidation
- Depression
- Psychotic condition

Obviously, you would want to figure out what is contributing most to the withdrawal before you implement some intervention or referral. The depression, for example, could be either biologically based or reactive to some situation in the child's life. Your job is not to diagnose this condition but merely to notice there is a problem, because early identification is the key to successful treatment. It has been estimated that up to 15% of school-age children are at least moderately depressed (Maag & Forness, 1998).

Besides referral, there are things you can do to help this student feel cared for and supported, most notably by addressing cognitive distortions (dysfunctional thinking patterns that exaggerate or distort reality). Such individuals may hold a number of self-defeating beliefs that can be disputed:

| Dysfunctional Belief | Intervention |
| --- | --- |
| There's no hope. | You are choosing to give up. |
| I'll never get better. | Never? There isn't the slightest possibility? |
| It's their fault. | You have no responsibility for this at all? |
| This is terrible. | You mean it's uncomfortable. |
| This always happens. | Every time? Never an exception? |
| I can't do it. | Can't? You mean you won't. |

These challenges are intended not to create debates or arguments but merely to help the student examine the extent to which he or she is distorting reality, exaggerating the situation, and denying personal responsibility. Rather than blaming others by externalizing the problem, the goal is to restore internal strength.

If depression is a "quiet" problem, a much louder manifestation occurs when the sense of hopelessness leads to suicidal gestures or attempts. Whether a cry for help or a genuine effort at self-destruction, such incidents become devastating for everyone in the school.

It is important to separate the reality from the misconceptions about suicide. Capuzzi (1998) highlights a few of the myths:

- When kids talk about killing themselves, they rarely do so.
- Suicides occur without warning.
- Don't talk about it directly because it may give kids the idea.

As with almost all of the troubled students you deal with, it helps to listen carefully and empathetically. In potentially life-threatening situations such as this, you will want to look for risk factors:

1. History of suicide in the family

2. A definite plan

3. The means to carry out the plan

4. Expressed helplessness and despair

5. Fantasies of revenge and punishment

6. Previous attempts

If you suspect there might be some risk, you must refer the child immediately to a counselor for assistance. Be sure to follow up on the child afterward to make certain that help and support were provided.

## Those Who Are Severely Impaired

This group includes those children who cannot cooperate with your best efforts to help them because of some underlying organic or physiological problem. This could be the result of an underlying neurological problem, such as an attention deficit disorder or a mental illness, or it could be related to substance abuse. In spite of best intentions to change their behavior, such children demonstrate a degree of impulsivity and erratic conduct that makes it difficult for them to comply with defined norms. It is not that they are deliberately trying to create problems in class; it is just that their behavior is not within personal control.

Felipe is an absolutely delightful young man. He is charming, bright, and extremely talented as a musician. He also claims that doing well in school is important to him, although his attendance is inconsistent and he often falls asleep in class. During your interactions with him, you have found him to be highly motivated and engaging. You are perplexed, however, about why his behavior has not changed even though he appears so willing and cooperative.

Later you learn that he lives at home with his parents, grandmother, and three older siblings, all of whom are alcoholics. Parties rage well into the night. He often takes part in the festivities—staying up late drinking most nights, waking the next morning with a hangover. There is no way that he can attend school on a regular basis and perform successfully as long as he drinks alcohol. No teacher or counselor in the world can help him until he abstains from all alcohol or until his home environment is changed.

## Those Who Are "At Risk"

This term has been applied so generally that it can refer to children in imminent danger of abuse, those who are especially vulnerable to substance abuse, those who are on the verge of leaving school, or those who come from dysfunctional families (Webb, 1992). For our purposes, we are concerned with those children who are especially likely to develop behaviors disruptive to themselves or others. These are kids who may not yet be identified as challenging or difficult, but for whom there is a great probability that problems may very well develop. Box 2.1 summarizes some of the most common symptoms of troubled youth.

What makes this group of students so challenging is that because they have not yet developed problems, their motivation to change anything is minimal. "So what if all my brothers and sisters are drug dealers and my parents are both heavy users? That ain't gonna happen to me."

## The Aggressive Student

"Asshole."

"Excuse me?" the teacher replied, not at all certain he'd heard correctly. For gosh sakes, this was a second grader.

"Nothin'."

The kid had just stabbed a little girl in the seat in front of him with a pen. The crying victim had been carted off to the nurse's office. The rest of the children had become agitated in the process.

The teacher knelt down to the boy's level, looking him in the eyes. "May I ask why you did that?"

"Didn't do nothin'! Leave me alone!" With that, the boy launched himself forward with his body, knocking the teacher over. Before the teacher could recover, the kid had already pushed through the gathering crowd of children watching the confrontation, making another child cry in the process.

**Box 2.1** Symptoms of Troubled Youth

| | |
|---|---|
| Agitation | Absenteeism |
| Attention difficulties | Isolation or withdrawal |
| Sexual promiscuity | Substance abuse |
| Drop in school performance | Changes in behavior |
| Suicidal thoughts | Impulsive behavior |
| Weight loss or gain | Lethargy or fatigue |
| Frequent illnesses | Physical complaints |
| Attention-seeking behavior | Loss of interest or pleasure |
| Defiance | Atypical volatile moods |
| Expressed hopelessness | Frequent conflicts with others |

There is no more difficult challenge for teachers today than dealing with children who are physically and verbally aggressive, even potentially violent. In the aftermath of school shootings, at a time when even elementary-age children bring weapons to school, fully prepared to use them on anyone who gets in the way, any potentially threatening student must be taken seriously. There is risk of harming not only the learning environment but also the emotional and physical safety of others.

Close to half a million children each year are victims of assault (Long, 1992). In any given year in American schools, there are over 4,000 rapes, 11,000 attacks involving lethal weapons, and 200,000 fights. One in seven teens admitted they carried a weapon with them, most commonly a knife (National Center for Education Statistics, 1998). As if those statistics aren't alarming enough, consider that three fourths of all students in one study admitted that they had been bullied at some time in their school careers, and all but 10% of them reported negative side effects, ranging from mild ones such as apprehension and avoidance to severe effects such as depression, social phobia, withdrawal, and suicide attempts (Hazler, Hoover, & Oliver, 1993).

There are a number of reasons to account for the rise in violence, but certainly one significant factor has been the increased presence of death, murder, and graphic violence in the media. Any child looking for attention or who wishes to enact fantasies of revenge can emulate what has been seen on television shows, movies, nightly news, and in true crime books.

Even more common than the dramatic acts of violence that attract publicity are the almost daily onslaughts of verbal abuse, disrespect, and incivility. In many cases, such behavior is not only effective in getting one's needs met, but is sometimes the ideal strategy for exercising power. Let's face it, intimidation works extremely well. Students who "advertise" themselves as explosive, impulsive, angry, and violent are able to get their way more often than not. Other students stay out of the way; friends allow them privileges to avoid confrontations; and teachers, even if they are not afraid of provoking such individuals, may still be reluctant to demand very much from them.

In Box 2.2, possible meanings and causes of violent behavior are listed, including the last item, which you might find perplexing: learning disorders. Indeed, sometimes the student's frustration and lashing out can stem from problems that make the school environment a perceived battleground.

In a stunning example of the impact such learning problems can have, Sammy "The Bull" Gravano, ex-hitman and highest-ranking member of the Mafia to ever testify against the mob, talks about what drove him to a life of crime and violence. Granted, this may very well be an elaborate rationalization blaming the system for his own immoral, ruthless conduct, but his story nevertheless has the familiar ring of truth.

A victim of dyslexia during a time before it was diagnosed and understood, Sammy was held back in fourth grade. He was viewed as slow, probably retarded. He was humiliated by his school experience, and this was made worse by how he was treated as a dummy by his teachers. As a result, he certainly drove more than a few of his teachers crazy.

Because Sammy couldn't win approval for being bright and precocious (which he was), he next tried the role of "class clown," which was also unappreciated. Then he turned to using his fists to

---

**Box 2.2** Possible Meanings of Aggressive Behavior

- Exercise in power
- Demand for respect
- Effect of what is modeled at home
- Normative behavior in peer group
- Impulse disorder triggered by frustration or perceived threats
- Calculated and strategic manipulation
- Retribution or revenge
- Explosive personality/temperament
- Learned problem-solving strategy
- Learning disorder

---

win respect and immediately found himself at the very top of the food chain.

"It's not like I was trying to impress these guys, or anything like that," the killer says about the new status he enjoyed as a result of terrorizing others, "but when I fought and got a pat on the head from them, it was a compliment" (Maas, 1997, p. 16).

There was one teacher who managed to get through to Sammy, although obviously the effects didn't last. He gave Sammy a chance, treated him with respect and kindness, and spent time with him showing him alternative ways to solve problems. "One time, he told me, 'Sammy, I've gotten to know you. You're far from being stupid. You just don't try anymore. Try for me'" (Maas, 1997, p. 15).

Apart from how annoying it can be to deal with overly aggressive students, they also have a huge impact on the classroom and larger school environment. They contribute to an atmosphere of mistrust and fear, for if students fear ridicule, teasing, verbal abuse, and physical attacks, they are hardly in the best state for revealing themselves in an authentic way. Anxiety is also strongly detrimental to students' learning. Some children will not even venture into the bathrooms during the day for fear they will be beaten up.

Aggressive behavior can even become contagious, triggering responses from other students and igniting increased conflict. In a sense, such children demonstrate how effective power and intimidation can be. Unless this behavior is checked, things can deteriorate rather quickly.

A number of sources (see Bemak & Keys, 2000; Johns & Carr, 1995) offer constructive strategies for handling violent and aggressive youth, as well as preventing such behavior in the future:

1. As with all other difficult students, work on your relationship first. If you have some semblance of dialogue and respect between you, it is far more likely that you can influence things.

2. Whenever possible, handle the problem yourself rather than calling in others, which risks compromising your authority.

3. Don't threaten the child unless you are prepared to follow through on what you say you will do.

4. Make your rules clear, with consequences specified, and enforce them consistently.

5. If possible, handle censures privately so there is no public loss of face.

6. Don't resort to sarcasm, humiliation, screaming, or other attempts that exacerbate the conflict. Stay calm and model the kind of behavior you would like to see others develop.

7. Whenever the aggressive student does manage to behave properly (however rare that might be), reinforce that positive contribution.

8. Pay attention to what the acting out is saying. Are your lessons boring? Irrelevant? Too difficult? Too predictable?

9. Censure the aggressive behavior, but not the individual.

10. Anticipate and prevent problems before they occur. Study the situation carefully. When, where, how, and with whom do the outbursts take place? What signals an impending explosion? What are the circumstances most likely to lead to trouble?

11. Take the time to figure out what the behavior means. What needs are being met? How is this student frustrated? What doesn't he or she understand?

12. Teach alternative ways of getting needs met, as well as conflict resolution skills.

13. Introduce and enforce values of shared community and safety.

14. What is the student really communicating? ("I'm angry." "I'm hurt." "I feel ignored.")

15. How does the aggressive behavior fit into the larger context of this person's life? Is the student in a gang? What is being modeled at home?

16. What have you been doing (or not doing) that makes the problem better or worse?

Among all the problems presented in this book or that you will ever encounter, aggression and bullying are probably the most serious. As I've said, there is nothing that can destroy the learning environment more swiftly than fear. When you find yourself in the middle of some aggressive act, it is important to appear calm and confident (see Box 2.3).

Your first priority is to protect the safety of students in the class and also to protect yourself from harm. After the situation is neutralized, consult with the offender in such a way as to ensure that such an event does not occur again. If needed, refer for outside help to the counselor, administrator, or police. Finally, be sure to debrief such situations with your class, as other students are likely to have a lot of stuff churned up as a result of the disturbance.

MacGrath (1998) suggests that in some circumstances an angry outburst can become material for an object lesson or teaching point. Students can be encouraged to talk about their own anger, when it arises, and how they've attempted to deal with it effectively. The focus should no longer remain on the angry student but should be on everyone's experience. A sample of directions you might give is as follows:

1. Write a story about someone who becomes very angry and tries to deal with the feelings.

2. Act out several scenes in which students have been provoked to the point of anger. Experiment with alternative ways of responding.

3. Talk about the constructive and destructive uses of anger and indignation throughout history.

4. Have students share in small groups the last time they lost control of themselves.

5. Ask for examples in class of when students have had a recent experience of losing control.

6. Use self-disclosure and modeling to talk about a time when you became angry.

7. Offer a unit on the psychology of emotions in general and anger in particular.

8. With partners, brainstorm a list of the negative side effects that result from anger, as well as the possible benefits.

9. Teach a lesson on assertiveness training, highlighting the differences between aggression, passivity, and assertiveness.

---

**Box 2.3** When Facing an Angry Student

1. Take deep breaths to stay calm.
2. Talk to yourself internally.
3. Think before you react.
4. Ask yourself what is really going on.
5. Consider the options available.
6. Speak firmly but softly.
7. Calm the student down.
8. Defuse the situation.
9. Process the experience.

10. Assign books or movies in which anger is a major theme.

A similar number of options exist for *any* critical incidents or problematic behaviors that arise in class.

## Those Who Push Your Buttons

This last group is actually the most common. It is not solely the students' behavior that drives us crazy but also the feelings and reactions that their actions elicit in us. In other words, some students do not just come to us as obstructive or resistant: We make them that way.

I recall one instance in which a preschool child was initially reluctant to comply with a reasonable request to clean up a mess she had made. There was something about the way she defied me that really started a slow burn. Actually, I do not think she was as much defying me as she was practicing some new assertiveness skills, and therein lies the problem: I took this little altercation *very* personally. I even think that I was seeing her not for who she was, but rather as another child she reminded me of who had once given me a hard time.

I spoke more caustically to this little girl than I needed to in order to make my point. Bless her heart—in turn, she decided that I was not going to order her around, so she became even more defiant. Before we knew it, we were both involved in a major conflict that could have easily been avoided if I had not overreacted to what I perceived as a challenge to my authority. It was not so much that she was a difficult child as that she was a confident young person who did not take kindly to being spoken to in a disrespectful manner. In all honesty, I made her far more difficult than she would have otherwise been.

# Questions to Ask Yourself

Children are difficult not only because of the ways they act but also because of how we interpret their behavior. Although there is some consensus about which children are among the most challenging for teachers, it is worthwhile for us to consider situations from other angles.

A number of questions might prove helpful in this regard:

- *Who experiences the child as difficult?* It is important to determine who actually "owns" the problem. Does everyone in this student's life experience him or her as difficult? If not, what might that say about the interactive effect that is going on?
- *How does the child view the situation?* A crucial strategy is to look at things from the other's point of view. In any conflict situation, there are always several different perspectives. You can bet that the child looks at you in much the same way that you view him or her.
- *How does his or her family view things?* What is their take on the situation? Because everyone is pointing fingers at everyone else as being the source of the difficulty, it is likely that the family will have someone else to blame.
- *How do the child's best friends view things?* This is a *very* interesting source of information. Often when children will not speak for themselves, their closest friends can describe things going on beneath the surface.
- *What precipitates the problem behavior?* What happens just before the problematic behavior arises? What are the situations and circumstances that are most likely to be associated with difficulties? Just as important, what are the exceptions, when the student does *not* act out?
- *What are the effects of this behavior?* What are the consequences of the student's behavior? I am talking not just about the negative effects but also the positive ones. Usually people act the ways they do because they enjoy some benefit.
- *What would be the consequences of changing the behavior?* If the student were to change his or her ways, what would result? Again, it is important to look not only at what would get better but also at what would become worse (perhaps the problem is a distraction from more serious problems).
- *What are some alternative ways to frame the problem?* What are some different ways in which you might look at things? How could you define the problem in a way that it might be more easily resolved?

- *What is your contribution to the conflict?* This is the most difficult question of all, because it forces you to look at your own
  behavior and what you might be doing to make matters worse.

These questions can help clarify why particular students seem so
difficult to work with. By placing their actions in a context that considers the circular causes and effects, you are able to see more clearly
why the behavior is so difficult to change and why these particular
students get under your skin.

To succeed with challenging students, it is critical to understand
exactly what is going on and why children are acting the way they are.
In the next chapter, we examine situations from two different angles—
one that explores the reasons why children act out and the other that
looks at the ways we sometimes make things far more difficult than
they need to be.

# CHAPTER 3

---

# Understanding Students' Challenging Behavior

O ne of the things that makes it difficult for us to deal with so-called challenging students is not understanding why they act the way they do. It seems incomprehensible to us that some children will go to such lengths to make life so difficult, for themselves and for us, when it would be so much easier to be cooperative. Why, for instance, would a student repeatedly neglect to turn in homework assignments that require at most 15 minutes per night, when the consequences involve severe punishment by parents and teachers? Why would a student create a disturbance that she knows is going to get her kicked out of school? Why would someone get in fights that he is certain he is going to lose? Why must students be so unpleasant and unreasonable when it seems so much easier to get along?

## They Are Doing the Best They Can

Before we can ever hope to reach challenging students, we must first understand why they are acting the way they are. All behavior, whether it is comprehensible to you or not, persists because it is helpful in some way to that person: It has some functional value or some protective role in the family.

If the child were not getting something out of the behavior, if it were not serving him or her in some way, he or she would do something else. Granted, what the child is getting may seem mysterious, or even perverse; nevertheless, all behavioral patterns that continue are being reinforced in some way, if not by friends then by some inner reward.

Medical professionals discovered long ago that certain patients recover from surgery far more quickly than others. In some cases, people who should improve rather routinely instead languish in their beds and demonstrate only the slightest improvement, even when there is no medical reason to account for this slow recovery. Apparently, some patients receive "secondary gains" from their behavior. They have good reasons for not getting better sooner. They enjoy the benefits of being in the role of the sick person—the attention they are getting, the excuse to remain helpless, the legitimate reason for not rejoining a life that in some ways feels abhorrent. Until nurses and doctors address these underlying reasons for such patients' slow recovery, significant progress remains unlikely.

This same conceptual model may be applied to the school situation if you are interested in understanding the reasons why some of your most uncooperative students are acting in particular ways. Even if this perspective does not suggest alternative methods of intervention, it sure makes it easier to respond objectively, because you will not be taking their behavior so personally. Challenging students are not doing anything *to you;* rather, they are just doing their best to help themselves or their families.

An 11-year-old was referred to me as his counselor because he had been caught setting off the fire alarm at school. His parents were puzzled, as were his teachers, because prior to this incident he had been a model student. I spent a few sessions with this child that were most productive. He seemed contrite and cooperative. He acknowledged his wrongdoing and promised never to do anything like that again. His grateful parents called and praised my miraculous work.

A few weeks later, the parents called again. I had been so helpful with their 11-year-old that they wondered if I might be willing to see their eldest son as well. At 17, he was a senior in high school and a star on several athletic teams. Lately, his coaches were benching him because of his defiant behavior. This was hurting not only the boy but also the team, which was losing out on his talent.

Again I was surprised at how quickly things proceeded. It took all of three sessions to explore what was going on. The boy admitted he didn't quite know what the problem was, but he was determined to be more cooperative with his coaches. He thanked me for my help and then reported to his parents that he was now much improved.

At this point, I must admit, I was feeling very impressed with myself. Ordinarily, I had never been this successful in such a brief period of time with two children who seemed to be presenting such puzzling problems. Nevertheless, I assumed that my counseling skills were just getting better and better.

When this family called again, asking me if I might see their middle son about some fits of rage he was throwing around the house, I readily agreed. By now, I'm sure that you are nodding your head smugly, seeing the pattern that I had missed—these boys were acting out at school and home for some reason that had to do with their family situation. I must admit that it was weeks later before it occurred to me to work with the parents instead of the children. It took all of 5 minutes to discover that this couple was on the verge of divorce. I also learned that as long as one of their children was having trouble, they presented a united, helpful front. Once things calmed down, however, then they would both resort to their usual screaming and threatening to walk out. Unconsciously, there was a conspiracy among their children to take turns developing problems as a way to keep the family intact.

In many situations you will see in school, children act out not because they necessarily enjoy being bad, but because their behavior is somehow functional or useful to them or others. Your job will be to figure out what benefits result from their behavior before you can hope to alter the pattern.

Although the underlying problem in the family mentioned earlier became obvious, in many circumstances it is quite difficult to gather enough information to see the larger picture. For this reason, Peeks (1992) emphasizes how important it is to meet with the parents of difficult children so you can not only enlist their support but also read some of what is going on in the family. I am not suggesting that you have either the time or the training to do some form of family intervention, but such explorations will better prepare you to understand what is going on behind the scene.

Applying the "systemic" model that is now quite popular among therapists, it is assumed that the child's symptoms actually help the family make some organizational transition. Table 3.1 lists the kinds of problems that you might detect.

Challenging students act in ways that appear disruptive, resistant, and noncompliant because of an agenda, often beyond their own awareness, that is fortified by their behavior. Specifically, such students enjoy the following secondary gains from behavior that we label as difficult.

*The student feels empowered.* If you feel powerless in your life, at the mercy of adults who control your freedom and at the whim of circumstances that seem grim and without hope, what better way to maintain a sense of personal control than to disrupt the balance of a teacher?

Teachers and counselors are godlings. We are the ones with the authority to decide what goes on within our domain, even who gets to go to the toilet or get a drink of water. According to our preferences and moods, we determine who goes to the blackboard, who gets to speak, and what happens when someone does something we do not like. Just imagine how powerful indeed a child must feel if he or she can get to us, really get under our skin. Sure, there are some nasty side effects to making a teacher mad, but for those who perceive themselves as having nothing to lose, a censure or trip to the principal's office is a small price to pay.

Students who revel in their disruptive power are living in a culture in which such nihilistic acts are respected, if not actively reinforced. As one student might describe this attitude:

> Yeah, I'm in trouble a lot. So what? No big deal. I'd rather destroy things on my own terms than be a victim of someone else, especially a teacher. I mean, I can't talk back to my father or he'd kill me; he probably would. I can't fight with my friends too much or they won't have anything to do with me. But a teacher? What can *you* do? Kick me out of your room? So what? It makes me feel good to think that I can make you miserable right along with me.

**Table 3.1** Home-Life Factors That Can Exacerbate In-School Problems for Students

| Disasters | Transitions |
|---|---|
| Natural disasters (floods, earthquakes) | Family development (child leaving home) |
| Financial or legal problems | Individual development |
| Tragedies (death, victimization) | Reorganization following divorce or remarriage |
| **Organizational Disputes** | **Hierarchical Disorder** |
| Disagreements with school | Intrusive grandparents |
| Problems with community agencies | Unhealthy family coalitions |
| Distractions from other family problems | Unequal parental power |
| **Discipline** | **Marital Conflict** |
| Lack of parental consensus | Ongoing tension and conflict |
| Lack of boundaries and clear rules | Covert battles with children in the middle |
| Inconsistent enforcement | Imminent divorce |

Perverse reasoning? Certainly. Counterproductive if your priority is learning? Assuredly so. However, if your intention is to feel powerful and if you are part of a culture that sees teacher authority types as part of the mainstream establishment that seeks to dominate and control people like you, there is tremendous satisfaction in getting your licks in while you can.

*The student enjoys attention.* Ask a student why she keeps being so uncooperative and, if she is honest, she might tell you, "Because it's fun!" Indeed, it *is* fun, in a way, to enjoy the attention of your peers. If you can't win this spotlight in other ways, say, through your athletic prowess, academic achievement, or fancy clothes, stirring things up in class is not a bad option.

In the culture of some students, there is much to be gained from drawing any attention to yourself. As comedian and ex-class clown George Carlin explained in one of his routines, if he wasn't learning much of value in school, why not deprive others of their education as well? He could not make it as a scholar or a football player, but boy, could he make kids laugh.

*The student avoids responsibility for his or her behavior.* Some students are threatened by our attempts to reach out to them. Even if they wanted to excel in their schoolwork, their peer and sometimes family cultures would sabotage their efforts. They feel much ambivalence. On the one hand, they may find us engaging on a personal level and feel intrigued by things we are doing in class. On the other hand, if they let themselves be drawn in by us, if they were to cooperate with our plans, they would lose status among their peers, which is far more important.

One student explains,

> I once brought schoolwork home to do and everyone made fun of me. My friends thought I'd totally lost it. My mom didn't like the idea that I might be smarter than her. My brother and sisters teased me. Forget it. No way I could do any work at home.

The scenario unfolds in which the student tests the teacher in some way—becomes challenging, refuses to cooperate, or otherwise draws attention in distracting ways. The teacher has no choice but to intervene. The student then feels misunderstood and unfairly treated. Furthermore, the teacher is blamed for the problems: "Hey, why should I put up with this crap? I never get a break."

The payoff to this way of thinking is that the student is not at fault for the troubles. In addition, such a strategy keeps the teacher from getting too close.

*The student is able to maintain the status quo and ward off perceived threats.* As is implied from the previous secondary gain, the student may seek to distract the teacher (and others). This is a recurrence of the theme of destroying things on your own terms: "If you really knew me, you would probably reject me. I am rejecting you first, though, so you can't hurt me."

A predictable sequence of events ensues: (a) The teacher reaches out to the student; (b) the student feels threatened by the overture and so withdraws; (c) the teacher feels rebuffed and so backs off; (d) the student acts provocatively to regain attention on his or her own terms; (e) the teacher steps in to set limits; (f) the student feels victimized and misunderstood, escalating the disruptive behavior; (g) the teacher increases the levels of attempted control. And so on. The conflict eventually reaches the point where both parties feel misunderstood.

The teacher thinks, "Why should I even try with these kids? I have done everything I can to reach out to this child, and all he has done is try to hurt me."

The student thinks, "All of these people are alike. I knew I shouldn't trust any of them. First she gets on my case and starts nagging me. Then when I try to be myself more she cuts me off. No sense in even trying."

Neither teacher nor student has the foggiest idea of what the other person is all about. Each of them feels justified in writing the other one off.

Only by understanding these underlying dynamics of the challenging student's behavior, as well as the larger context of his or her family and peer culture, are effective efforts to be helpful possible. Until you can answer the question "What exactly is this student getting out of this behavior?" interventions are likely to be misguided. This is only the first step in trying to work through conflicts with challenging students.

## Additional Functions of Conflict

Given the headaches and heartaches that we normally associate with conflict, whether it is with a student, a colleague, or a family member, we do not often consider how such interpersonal skirmishes provide a number of benefits. These are advantages not only for students who may be the initiators of the disagreement but also for those who exacerbate the problems for reasons of their own. Before you react defensively—"What, me? How dare you suggest that I do anything to keep conflicts going; I certainly have enough to worry about that I don't need to make matters worse!"—I'd like you to consider some of the positive things that can result from conflict.

*Conflict releases tension.* When tempers are flaring, emotional energy is being expressed. There is an intensity to conflict in which both participants are discharging pent-up feelings. One teacher explains this reaction:

> I don't like one of the other guys I have to work with. He is pushy. He always tries to boss me around. Even worse, he doesn't really know what he is doing, and I'm always cleaning up after him, covering for his mistakes.
>
> There are many times that I would really like to tell him off, put him in his place, but I never do. I just swallow my frustration and go about my work. So there I am feeling angry as hell, and in walks this student with a note telling me that I'm supposed to take care of some problem. The kid mouths off to me, but I've had just about enough for the day: I give it right back to him. Before we know it, we are yelling at each other. I don't know if he felt any better afterward, but I sure did!
>
> We both blew off a little steam and then we were able to sit down and figure out something to do. I apologized first, and that made it easier for him to tell me that he was sorry, too. It was actually a great way to start, although I certainly would never have planned it that way.

*Conflict maintains distance.* Another function that conflict serves is to control just how close one will let him- or herself get to others, psychologically speaking. Some children, who are not used to being involved with adults as compassionate and caring as we are, feel vulnerable and confused by their feelings. They have little experience in such healthy relationships and feel unprepared to deal with them.

One of the most effective and efficient ways to push away a well-meaning teacher or other helpful adult is to create some sort of dramatic conflict. For example, I recall one 4-year-old with whom I had been working to help control her temper tantrums. She loved our sessions together because I was one of the few adults in her life who responded to her consistently. There were certain aspects of her behavior that I would not tolerate, but I was always calm and caring in the ways that

I would restrain her, never raising my voice. Over time, we came to care about one another very much, and this frightened her.

Every few weeks or so, she would deliberately provoke some argument. She would refuse to abide by the rules we had established. She would do something that she knew would upset me. At first, I wondered why she would deliberately try to do this, until I realized that in her own ingenious way she was keeping me from getting closer to her than she could handle.

*Conflict highlights issues of control.* In one way or another, conflict usually ends up being about who is going to get his or her way. Disagreements thus signal that both parties are trying their best to exert some sort of power over the other.

The teacher wants the student to abide by rules that she believes are important; the student has his own agenda—to be given the freedom to do things the way he prefers. The conflict between them is the inevitable result of two people determined to get their way. For reasons mentioned earlier, the student may actually enjoy the conflict, with the accompanying feelings of power; he feels little motivation to resolve things satisfactorily. He may not be getting exactly what he wants, but he is also keeping the teacher from getting her way as well. Although not an ideal solution, it certainly creates a respectable impasse for those who are not used to getting what they want very often.

*Conflict underscores underlying issues to be resolved.* Conflicts get our attention. They are disagreeable experiences that churn up a number of negative feelings. As such, they act as motivators to resolve whatever is really disturbing to people.

A teacher was about halfway through a parent conference, going through the usual spiel about how their daughter's low achievement was a reflection more of poor motivation than of lack of ability, when the father and mother erupted into a dispute about whose fault it was that their child was a failure. Interestingly, however, they didn't actually talk about their daughter but rather about whose turn it was to pick up groceries on the way home. The teacher, caught in the middle, felt like he was watching a tennis match, so well rehearsed were their respective "shots" at one another. During an opportune pause in the argument, he offered that perhaps what they were really upset about was how powerless they felt to change their child's behavior. Their conflict only drew attention to the degree of their feelings of helplessness and frustration.

## When Biology Has Its Say

Most of what we have been discussing so far implies that difficult students drive you crazy because they are somehow making a choice to be obstructive, resistant, or ornery. It is also important to recognize that about 12% of children have some recognizable brain disorder (Koplewicz, 1996). These are children with attention deficit and hyperactivity disorders, obsessive-compulsive disorders, Tourette's syndrome, enuresis, depression, chronic anxiety or panic disorder, autism, schizophrenia, and other progressive neurological disorders. Each of these disorders can result in children's shame, isolation, anger, frustration, and lack of self-control. They all present behavior that is unpredictable, provocative, puzzling, and unmanageable. Furthermore, for every one of these kids, there is at least one parent and teacher who blames him- or herself for being unable to exert effective control. Teachers most often think that parents are the problem. Parents are just as likely to blame teachers. It is this blame and fault finding that actually prevent us from dealing effectively with the problems (DiGiulio, 2000; Kottler, 1994).

There are times when it is extremely important to recognize that the problems you are encountering with a student may not be within his or her control. If you even suspect that such might be the case, you must make a referral to an appropriate medical specialist to check out the possible organic condition.

## Creating Difficult Students

I have mentioned several times already that conflicts in general, and disputes with students who drive you crazy in particular, are almost always the result of some interactive effect in which both parties make some contribution to the problem (Kottler, 1994).

You may be skeptical that this is really the case, because it so often seems that you are only doing your job in the best way you know and that some students just seem to enjoy trouble. The interesting thing, however, is that when you talk to these supposed trouble-makers, you find that they feel just as misunderstood, unappreciated, and victimized as you do. It is not so much a matter of figuring out who is right, or who is to blame, as it is of simply recognizing that disputes require all participants to make some changes.

Most often, you encounter difficulties that are caused (or exacerbated) by your own actions (or inactions) under the following circumstances:

*When You Are Missing Information.* A student may appear to be unusually reticent and resistant to your best efforts to be helpful. Then you learn that she has been betrayed before by someone she trusted. Further, you learn that one of the messages she received growing up was not to trust *anyone* in a helping role.

*When You Hold Invalid Assumptions.* You assume that a child has a problem with authority. After all, in response to your most innocuous requests for compliance, you encounter marked stubbornness. This assumption is challenged after discovering that what appears to be hostility to authority is actually quite a sensible defense against further physical and sexual abuse, which she suffers at home.

*When You Don't Do Something Very Well.* There are times when, as a result of something you say or do, you create difficulties where none previously existed. When you fail to provide adequate structure or clear enough instructions, or when you ask students to do things that are beyond their capability, you create frustration that leads to other undesirable side effects. When you cut a student off, censure someone, or otherwise show behavior that is *perceived* as disrespectful, you may have created a difficult student. When you misread cues or embarrass a student (even though you had the best of intentions), you may have made an enemy, or at least someone who no longer feels cooperative toward you.

The problem is not in making mistakes, which are inevitable. Students give us the benefit of the doubt when they know we are trying our hardest to understand them and treat them fairly. They are especially forgiving when we can acknowledge our errors and misjudgments.

Nevertheless, we spend an awful lot of time complaining to one another about how awful certain students are without looking at our own contributions to the conflicts. The question we should be asking is not "What is wrong with this student who is driving me crazy?" but "What might I have done to exacerbate these difficulties?"

Just as students can be labeled "difficult," so too can teachers. In one sense, perhaps there are no difficult students. After all, that is simply a judgment on the part of a teacher about behavior that is misunderstood. As I've said earlier, even the most belligerent child is acting in a particular way because he or she is getting something useful from such behavior.

## Multiple Viewpoints

I hear teachers, parents, principals, and counselors say all the time, "I just don't know what's wrong with these kids today. What makes them act so badly?" Of course, in their own discussions when they are left alone, children ask themselves a similar question about adults: "How can they be so stupid and out of it?"

There is a simple answer to why so-called difficult children act the way they do: It works for them. We may feel angry and indignant because their behavior seems unreasonable and dysfunctional, but that is only because we aren't looking at things from *their* viewpoint—which is that they are just doing the best they can. If they knew how to do something else that worked better for them, they would do that instead. Box 3.1 summarizes reasons why students are experienced as difficult.

Of course, our job is to teach them more socially appropriate alternatives. To do that, however, requires us first to understand why they act as they do or what they are getting out of those strategies. Second, and just as important, we must examine not only *their* behaviors, motives, and internal reactions, but our own as well. Conflict, after all, usually involves the contributions of two parties who are both acting stubbornly.

**Box 3.1** Why Students Are Difficult

- They don't know what is expected.
- They lack the skills or ability to do what you want.
- They desire attention, respect, and approval.
- They enjoy exercising power and control.
- They have a low tolerance for frustration.
- Influences at home or in their peer group reinforce their behavior.
- Their physical or psychological safety is threatened.
- They may be victims of trauma or abuse.
- They are bored.
- They have an emotional, neurological, or learning disorder.

# CHAPTER 4

## What They Do to Make You Crazy

Your worst nightmare walks in the door. This child gets to you like fingernails scraping on a blackboard, like a piece of spinach caught between your teeth, like a dull ache that won't go away. Who is this student?

Each of us has a secret list of students we consider most difficult—a list based not so much on what they do as on the ways we react to their behavior. Something gets in the way of our feeling particularly empathic and charitable toward them. We feel ourselves becoming impatient, rigid, argumentative, even unreasonable with them in ways we never would with anyone else. We spend an inordinate amount of time thinking about these children, much of it unproductive. We whine and complain to colleagues, family members, and anyone else who will listen about how tough we have it. We tell "war stories" about the latest battles that we have fought to a standstill. Furthermore, if we were totally honest, we would have to admit that there is just something about these students that rubs us the wrong way.

## Separating Students and Behavior

Although the primary focus of this book is on those individual students who trouble you the most, there are also particular difficult behaviors that almost any student might engage in on occasion. These amount to those irresponsible actions that take up an extraordinary amount of time and energy by teachers, counselors, and administrators to curb the discipline problems.

The "Top 10" behavior problems that drive teachers and administrators the most crazy on a regular basis include the following (McEwan & Damer, 2000):

- Leaving school grounds without permission
- Physical aggression toward others
- Disturbing others in class, in hallways, or on school grounds
- Using disrespectful or abusive language
- Destruction or inappropriate use of school materials
- Talking inappropriately or without permission
- Being out of one's seat during class
- Resistance to or noncompliance with a teacher's requests
- Failure to work independently
- Disorganized behavior, such as inability or unwillingness to complete work in a timely manner

Some students you encounter might engage in these annoying behaviors sporadically, but it is the chronic offenders who really test your limits. They get to you because they don't seem to be interested in changing those behaviors that you most need altered in order to do your job. Either they don't see any reason to change or you haven't yet discovered the magic solution to make that happen. Far more likely, there are other things going on that "reward" their disruptive actions, making it more fun and satisfying to continue along their present course. In many cases, it's even worth a few threats and scoldings from an annoyed teacher to proceed according to the same pattern. In some instances, this is just the icing on the cake that makes these actions even more attractive to them: Not only do such students get to do what they want, they also get to upset the teacher at the same time! That's a heck of a winning combination.

## Those Who Don't "Fight Fair"

Although some students become challenging for us to work with because of our issues as much as theirs, some of them earn the label "resistant" through their own hard work. These are the dilemmas we face when involved with someone who will not "fight fair," the type of student who resorts to sometimes ingenious strategies to appear cooperative but who actually is doing everything possible, consciously or not, to sabotage things.

I remember seeing one such individual in counseling. I assume she was referred to me in the first place because other people in her life were banging their heads against walls in frustration. For the longest time I could not figure out what Candy's problem was. Here was a young woman who presented herself as the prototype of the perfect client—she was sugary sweet, appeared extremely cooperative, would do almost anything I asked of her, and was effusive in her gratitude for how much I was helping her. The only problem was that although she was a model citizen in my office, Candy was a skilled provocateur in the jungles of her own world.

When I confronted her about this discrepancy, she decided to use her considerable talents to make my life as miserable as her own. Because she deduced quite accurately that helplessness was the key to driving me crazy, she expressed her tremendous rage toward the world and anger toward me by developing almost every set of symptoms I had ever read about. Then she would call me late at night and beg for help. Or she would have car trouble on the way to an appointment in which she was to report significant changes in her life. Sometimes she would just sit in my office, perfectly still, tears rolling down her face, and refuse to say a single word for the hour.

When I interpreted her behavior as unexpressed anger, Candy "punished" me by skipping the next two sessions altogether. When I confronted her on that passive-aggressive ploy, she sweetly acknowledged there might be some merit to the point ("Oh Dr. Kottler, sometimes you say the most insightful things"), bided her time, and then checked herself into the hospital. Candy asked that I apologize to her for being so mean before she would agree to comply with her treatment. And although over a period of years, with patience, compassion, and firm limit setting, she did improve significantly, she never once admitted that there was anything deliberate about her manipulative ploys.

Remember now, Candy and people just like her are walking around in the world. Younger versions of her are in your classes as students. Because they feel so little power in their lives, such individuals get a visceral thrill out of controlling your life as much as possible. Although few of the people you ever meet will manifest such extreme manipulative behavior and such severe emotional disturbance as Candy, most of us have encountered on more than a few occasions attempts by people to control us through manipulative gestures.

The main challenge in dealing with these people is that unless they are willing to fight fair—that is, to acknowledge their hostile feelings and express them appropriately—there is little we can do to work with them very effectively. That is why it is useless to try to change them or blame them: You will only escalate the struggle. Instead, direct your attention toward the three priorities that will be discussed in this and later chapters. First and foremost, protect yourself from collateral damage that results from their self-destructive ploys. Second, control what you do inside your own head so that you do not hurt yourself with remorse and blame. And third, identify accurately which manipulative strategy is being used, and respond with an appropriate counterresponse—not just externally, but internally as well.

## Protecting Yourself

Sigmund Freud was the first to suggest that a stance of neutral detachment is most helpful for maintaining enough distance from people who are acting out. His use of the couch in treatment, for example, was invented as much to increase his own comfort as it was to facilitate free association. Being able to sit outside of his clients' line of vision allowed him to remain more objective and out of the direct onslaught of their anger or frustration.

Detachment, which is essential to psychoanalytic relationships, is also helpful in other conflicted interactions. Taking a step back allows us to disengage from the personal aspects of a conflict and remain clear enough to decide how to respond effectively without being distracted by our feelings of hurt and anger.

Note, for example, in the following heated interaction—between myself and a boy who was particularly obstructive and accusatory in his style— how I attempted to keep myself from getting sucked into the vortex of his anger:

Boy: How the hell can you live with yourself knowing you are such a fraud?

Me: You seem particularly angry at me today, even more so than usual. *(That's right. Keep the ball in his court.)*

Boy: There you go again with those shrink games. You must think I'm awfully stupid.

Me: *(Got me. Or I should say he is getting himself. This really isn't about me.)* I am not playing games with you. I just notice that as long as you keep the focus on me, you don't have to deal with your own stuff. *(There. That sounds right.)*

Boy: Very clever. You don't know what you are doing or how to help me, but you keep seeing me anyway.

Me: *(He's probably right about that.)* You want me to give you a guarantee? *(Oops. He is getting to me. Now I am being defensive. Take a deep breath. Back off.)* You seem awfully disappointed in me and what I've been able to do for you, but also disappointed in yourself. There is a lot at stake for you in this relationship. *(Much better. In order to help him, I've got to stay calm.)*

Boy: Look, we can go around and around about this forever. Since *I* am the client here, I would just as soon talk about why you can't help me.

Me: *(He is tapping into my own doubts about my work. Sensitive soul that he is, he knows I wonder about whether I am really doing anything to help him.)* If you don't feel that you are getting help from me, perhaps you'd like to see someone else? *(Damn! He got me. Now I am really defensive.)*

Boy: Not so fast. You think you can drop me just because I'm giving you a hard time? What's the matter? Can't you stand the heat?

If I'm ever to help this person, it is imperative that I not allow myself to become emotionally threatened to the point that I start defending myself or attacking him in retribution. This is, naturally, very difficult to do when the other person is as skilled as this student at finding vulnerable areas to exploit. On the other hand, it is often helpful to realize that you might not be the only person who is having trouble getting along with this individual.

## Pushing Our Buttons

Each of us has unresolved issues that are constantly coming to the surface at inopportune times. Most of us actually entered the education field for reasons other than pure altruism. Yes, we enjoy helping people and making the world a better place, but we are also seeking to save ourselves in the process.

Some of the buttons that are pushed by certain students include the following:

- Fear of failure
- Secret feelings of incompetence, of being a fraud
- Feelings of helplessness, ineptitude, and impotence when we cannot make things better
- Memories of the most painful times of our own childhood
- Personal need for control

During those times when students do or say things that force us to look at our sore spots or to relive unresolved issues related to control, power, and authority, we react or, more likely, *overreact* to what is happening. What starts out as a little disagreement becomes a full-fledged battle of wills.

I know, for example, that I have great trouble with anger. When I was a kid, my parents fought a lot, and I did everything I could to hide from the emotional hurricanes that would hit my house at regular intervals. I pride myself on the control I have shown throughout my life to neither acknowledge nor express anger. When anyone acts angry toward me, I either pout or, if possible, get as far away as I can.

In my work with preschoolers, adolescents, and adults, I have inevitably encountered individuals who, at times, feel anger—toward themselves, toward classmates, and, most uncomfortably, toward me. During those times when a student has become enraged, or even just a little angry, I have not always responded in my best (or most professionally appropriate) manner. In some cases, if I had just let things run their course or shown some understanding of what the person might have been feeling, the situation would have resolved itself. Instead, because I felt so defensive and wounded by displays of anger, my tendency was often to quickly cut the student off. I have noticed time and time again that this was a turning point when an otherwise responsive student became challenging for me to deal with thereafter. To put it another way, we became difficult for one another because the relationship irrevocably changed. The part that is most difficult for me to own is that such a student did not start out being resistant to me and what we were doing in class or sessions: I helped to make the person that way by how I reacted to his or her behavior.

How do you know when a student is driving you crazy?

- When you spend an inordinate amount of time thinking about a particular child or complaining about him or her to others
- When you repeatedly find yourself misunderstanding a child and feeling misunderstood yourself by him or her
- When you are aware of feeling particularly frustrated, helpless, and blocked with a child
- When your empathy and compassion are compromised and you find it difficult to feel respectful and caring toward a child

Each of these symptoms may signal that you have lost your composure and objectivity, that your own unresolved issues may be getting in the way of being truly helpful to a particular student.

Therefore, if we are going to talk about so-called difficult students, we would be negligent if we downplayed our own tendencies to become difficult teachers. Where should you look for such vulnerable spots? The following are a few of the most common ones.

*Seeing Ourselves Mirrored.* There is no doubt that one of the most painful aspects of working with children—whether as a parent, teacher, or counselor—is that we must relive our own childhood over and over again. We see things every day that remind us of our own experiences in school. Sometimes we even see ourselves in the vision of a particular child.

When we experience students as being especially difficult, sometimes we are responding not just to who they are in the present but also to someone they remind us of. This, after all, is the hallmark of what is described as "countertransference," that distorted reaction that alters our perception of reality. Instead of seeing particular students as they are, we see ourselves or someone else they bring to mind. Let's face it—every kid we see reminds us of another one we have encountered before.

A reality check permits us to consider whether the extent to which a child appears to be difficult is really just our own exaggerated response to a distorted image. Of course, it takes an extraordinary amount of personal clarity and honest self-reflection to recognize this pattern. One teacher, for example, was finding himself especially annoyed with a third-grade bully who was terrorizing some of the other children. Rather than feeling the least amount of compassion or empathy for this child, the teacher was overidentifying with the victims to the extent that he kept trying to exact revenge, not only for the bully's present behavior but for all the bullying the teacher had ever suffered in his own life.

Some professionals would say that identifying this distortion and then counteracting it is very difficult, if not impossible, without years of intensive therapy and continual weekly supervision that is geared toward recognizing such issues as they emerge. Nevertheless, most of us are aware of primary personal issues that we have not yet fully resolved, even if we aren't yet prepared to resolve them.

*Haunted by the Past.* So, where are *you* most vulnerable? What are the major problems with which you have struggled throughout your life? Which patterns in your most conflicted relationships tend to repeat themselves again and again?

In my experience, it might be helpful to look at the extent to which you have fully resolved the following issues, most or all of which seem to be common for helping professionals:

- *Intimacy.* To what extent have you been able to create healthy, intimate relationships in your life? When you feel needy or stifled in other relationships, it is not unusual that such dynamics also play out in your sessions with clients.
- *Approval.* How well do you deal with things when other people do not give you the validation that you would prefer? You may find yourself doing things in sessions that have little to do with helping anyone other than yourself.
- *Power.* How well do you handle struggles when another person seeks to control you? Some student-teacher relationships become infused with conflict primarily because we persist in establishing that we are the ones in charge, even at the expense of reaching educational goals.

These are just a few of the hundreds of themes that play themselves out in our work every day. We are tested constantly—pushed to examine those issues that are often the most frightening for us to consider. And one theme, to which I referred earlier, can be particularly annoying and distressful.

It is one of our deepest, darkest secrets that most of us feel like frauds. Much of the time, we do not really know what we are doing in our work—we are improvising, sometimes even faking it. We don't know nearly as much as we pretend to know, even if students expect that we are endless sources of knowledge. During moments of honest self-reflection, we also admit that sometimes our primary motive is not to succeed but to avoid failure.

No matter how many students you have taught before, here sits this resistant child who will not respond to anything you do. She is a dramatic reminder of the limits of what you can do. She mocks you, not so much by her taunting but by her stubborn refusal to learn much of anything. A quiet but painful whisper in your head reminds you that you may have lost your magic. Maybe you can't reach her. Maybe you can't help anyone.

As long as the student stays stuck, you feel like a failure. Surely someone brighter and more capable than you are would know exactly what to do with this student. If only you had a master's or doctoral degree, or had attended one more workshop, or read a few more books, you would be able to help this person.

You shake your head, as if to clear your mind, and then say all the right things that you have heard before. There are limits to what you can do. It is the student's job to learn. You are taking too much responsibility for the outcome; you are overinvested. Yes, you nod your head—this is all true. But you still feel like a failure. You look at this kid, and she reminds you of how helpless and powerless you feel much of the time, despite your effective facade.

## How Failure Helps

Rather than disowning or denying the fear of failure, with its corresponding side effects, it might be useful to look at some of the benefits that failures bring. In fact, the very label of "failure" is a judgment with a very negative connotation. Yet failure is inevitable for any professional who takes risks, experiments with new ideas, and engages fully with the world.

There are actually a number of quite positive outcomes that can result from failure, depending on how you choose to deal with such situations.

*Failure promotes reflection.* It is during times of disappointment that you take time out to figure out what went wrong. You consider the situation with some objectivity. You deconstruct the steps of what occurred. And ideally, you learn from the situation so that you can improve your performance next time.

As a teacher, when everything goes according to plan, I don't give things much thought, just move on to the next task. But when there is some critical incident, something that goes poorly, I am forced to figure out what happened. I do this most often with one situation that plagues me constantly in graduate classes I now teach. There is always one student who rambles a lot, taking more than his or her fair share of allocated time. No matter how I attempt to intervene, softly or firmly, publicly or privately, I end up blowing the situation more often than not, making things worse. I have spent an incredible amount of time thinking about this scenario, talking about it with colleagues, precisely because I fail more often than I would prefer in managing this situation. In a sense, I feel grateful for the opportunity to become far more skilled in my teaching interventions.

*Failure stimulates change.* When things don't work out as expected, you are required to make adjustments, to stretch yourself in new ways. The alternative—continuing to do what doesn't work—will only get you in deeper trouble.

A first-grade teacher has been taking her kids on a field trip to a butterfly farm for years. She has noticed that over the last 2 years, the kids haven't been nearly as attentive, interested, and well behaved as they had been previously, yet she has persisted in scheduling this experience because of what she remembers were such positive experiences in the past.

Through reflection, the teacher now wonders if this field trip was ever that suitable for this age group. Maybe it isn't so much that the kids have changed as that now she is more observant of their behavior. But it wasn't until the last group of kids really started to act up that she finally realized that it was time to substitute an alternative experience that might be more engaging for the children.

*Failure encourages flexibility.* When one thing doesn't work, it is time to try something else. Imagine, for example, that a child with whom you are having difficulty continuously disrupts class with various antics that are not even very amusing to the other kids. What you normally do in such situations is politely but firmly point out that such behavior will not be tolerated. If that doesn't work (which it never has yet with this boy), you then raise your voice and censure him more forcefully. This seems to shut him up for a little while, but the effects never last very long.

If you are honest with yourself, you admit that you are failing miserably with this kid. Not only have you lost him, but you are also losing control of the class, not to mention yourself. But there is an opportunity that arises as well. This child is not your worst enemy; rather, he can be the means to get your attention on the fact that you are being too rigid in the way you operate. He is giving you clear feedback to which you are not paying attention.

If you ever expect to get through to this student, or at least to minimize his mischief and effects on others, it is clear you are going to have to demonstrate a lot more flexibility and creativity in your methods. You might not know yet what would work in this situation, but you sure know what will *not* work—and that is what you are already doing!

*Failure improves frustration tolerance.* Failure can help you to be not only more flexible but also more forgiving of yourself and others. Quite simply, there are some situations you will never control and some kids with whom you will never develop good relationships. As frustrating as this might be, you can feel sorry for yourself and become dispirited about it, or you can learn to accept your own limitations.

You would only need to look around your school to see a herd of walking burnouts who have allowed themselves to become discouraged and demoralized. Not only do they see themselves as failures, they can't imagine the possibility of anything else. You hear them in the teachers' lounge complaining a lot, talking about the good ol' days. You observe them huddling together, all those who have given up, supporting one another in their despondency and negativity.

Now, the really scary thing about all this is that *at one time they were just like you.* They were optimistic, enthusiastic, hopeful, and highly motivated. So, you've got to ask yourself: What happened?

This is a complicated question, but one part of the answer comes from their inability to manage their frustration and come to terms with their disappointments. The reality of this work (which they rarely told us in school) is that much of the time we are not going to get through to even the majority of kids. *Every* class is going to have students who drive us a little crazy. That is just the price we pay for the privilege of being teachers and enjoying the victories that we experience every day as well.

*Failure teaches humility.* Failure reminds you that you are human. You are fallible. You make mistakes and misjudgments. Every day.

You can either learn from your errors and improve yourself based on this valuable feedback or you can wallow in your disappointments.

Not a day goes by that you can't beat yourself up pretty good for something you did that wasn't as elegant, intelligent, or well intended as you had hoped. Oh well. Time to move on. The alternative is to become a burnout yourself, one of the walking wounded.

*Failure provides useful information.* When you try something, there are two possible outcomes: It works or it doesn't work. Instead of treating unsuccessful results as *failures,* a very strong label with its own baggage, you can instead think of them as useful feedback.

Instead of saying to yourself, "Damn, I sure blew that one!" you can instead think internally, "That's interesting how things turned out. I wonder what that means?" This attitude of embracing failure as valuable input allows you to look at what you're doing more critically and then to make changes according to what the situation calls for. *Failure is nothing more or less than feedback on the impact of any action.*

## Engaging the Challenging Student

When teachers, counselors, or administrators are stuck, the first place they like to start is with the student. During attempts at consultation or supervision, the professional wants to talk about what the student is doing or not doing or what can be done to change the student's attitudes and behavior. I have quite a different strategy in mind, one that starts with your own behavior first.

Whenever you feel at an impasse in your relationships with students (or anyone else, for that matter), I suggest that you begin with yourself by asking the following questions, which represent a summary of issues we have covered previously:

- *What personal issues of yours are being triggered by this encounter?* More likely than not, the student is challenging your sense of competence.
- *What expectations are you demanding of this student?* Often students act out because they are either unwilling or unable to do what you want. It may be time to reassess what you are asking and make changes in light of what might be more reasonable or realistic.

- *What are you doing to create or exacerbate the problems?* Look at your need for control and the ways you respond when you feel this control is being challenged. Are you pushing this student in ways that are designed to be genuinely helpful to him or her, or are such designs ultimately of more help to you?
- *Who does this challenging child remind you of?* To what extent might you be distorting what is going on with this student? In what ways might you be responding not to who he or she really is but to who you imagine the student to be, based on prior experiences with others?
- *Which of your needs are not being met?* It is not pleasant to admit that you have certain personal needs in your work—for example, that students not only learn but also feel grateful to you for your help, that they show appropriate deference, that they confirm your favorite theories about the way people should act, and that they laugh at your jokes.

The intent of questions such as these is to help you to examine thoroughly and honestly your own internal reactions to what is taking place. When you are stuck in a conflicted relationship, rather than blaming the student for being a particular way (about which you can do little), look first at what you might be doing to magnify the difficulties. Change born of self-reflection is actually far easier to effect, because it is within your control.

## How Can You Help Yourself?

No matter how many resources are available to help you with difficult students, there are still limits to what you can do. You are well aware that there are children who are not going to improve no matter what you do or, for that matter, what anyone else may do. They live in home environments that are so toxic that they are likely to be scarred for life. They have suffered traumas from which they will need years to recover—far longer than the meager time that you have to work with them. They show the early signs of what are called "personality disorders" (chronic, intractable, self-destructive interpersonal styles) that impair their ability to engage in healthy relationships. Or they are simply stubborn young people who are determined to make life miserable for themselves and anyone else they can capture in their web.

We also have to accept the fact that we just cannot help everyone we would like to, not just because of their limitations but because of our own. Each of us tends to work well with some kinds of people and not so well with others. We all have our sore spots, our areas of weakness. These include deficiencies in our skills. Some of us are better at lecturing or small-group work or one-on-one consultations. One teacher is especially effective in working with passive, withdrawn girls. Another has particular success working with rather raucous groups but struggles with those that are more conventional. Still another teacher works miracles in the classroom when presenting complex content units but bungles those that lack structure.

No matter how much we know and can do or how much experience we have had, we still have to accept the reality that no matter how hard we try, we cannot reach everyone. Under such circumstances, or whenever it appears that a positive outcome is not likely in spite of our best intentions and more inventive strategies, we would be well advised to work on ourselves as well as our students.

This principle is a major premise of my profession of counseling, that you cannot change other people—you can only change yourself. Teachers and counselors sometimes feel exempt from this idea. We feel special because of our training. We believe that we really can save children, get them to turn things around, even though they may not even have an interest in doing so. Sure enough, this strong belief in our own powers to help really can work miracles! Often, we are indeed able to get through to the most defiant children who refused to cooperate. But sometimes we must accept the limits of what is within our control. Under such circumstances, there is work we can do with ourselves (sometimes with a little help from a friend) to deal with unsatisfactory outcomes and irreconcilable conflicts.

## Don't Take the Conflict Personally

Some teachers have the propensity not so much to blame others for their problems but instead to place the full burden of responsibility on themselves. I, for one, can be guilty of just such tendencies. I would much prefer to feel that I am the one at fault for an impasse rather than the other person. By doing so, I feel powerful—that I have far more influence and control than is actually possible. This way, I get to delude myself that there is always something that I can do to get myself out of a sticky situation. I much prefer this level of distortion to feeling helpless because I am being poorly treated without my consent or participation.

Often, professionals like me need reminders that when students are being difficult, it is not so much something they are doing to us as something they are doing to themselves. Their acting out may be directed not toward us at all but rather toward that of which we are a reminder or symbol. We know all this intellectually, of course. It is interesting, however, how often we forget about this simple idea of transference when we persist in personalizing everything.

Time and again, when we become indignant or angry or feel unappreciated, abused, or misunderstood, it is because we are telling ourselves that this difficult child is making our lives miserable. It is as if we believe that such children stay up late at night plotting ways to get to us the following day. During moments of grand delusion, I even wonder if there might be a secret association for such people, the Association of Difficult Students, wherein they trade their favorite resistant methods, coach one another in ingenious strategies to stymie their teachers, and even exchange information on which of our soft spots to exploit. It certainly feels that way some days when we face a child who seems to be playing us like a virtuoso.

There are few things more helpful in such circumstances than reminding ourselves to stay calm, especially telling ourselves that what is going on is not personal. This is just business. The difficult student is doing his or her best to keep you off balance so you don't get too close. However much you do not like it, remember that he or she is not trying to get you as a person— even though it often feels that way.

## It Comes With the Territory

The staff lounge is a dangerous place to hang out because teachers and counselors spend so much time complaining about how poorly they are being treated. "These kids are so ungrateful!" "Let me tell you what this one little boy did to me today." "You think you've got it bad? Let me tell you what happened to me today." And so on. Staff barely listen to one another's stories because they are so busy thinking about what they will say next.

It sort of reminds me of the absurdity of staff members who work in the complaints department of a company getting together to whine about how people are always complaining to them. Jeez! It's their job to listen to complaints! If they object to those sorts of interactions, they should work somewhere else.

The same holds true for the job of being an educator. In a sense, difficult children come with the territory; it's why we exist in the first place. If every child could learn effortlessly, without the need for experts, there would be no need for teachers. It is senseless to complain about kids who aren't cooperating when those are exactly the people we have been prepared to help. These children do not yet know how to act any other way.

It is far easier to respond to such children with compassion, neutrality, and inner calmness when we realize that that is exactly what we are trained and paid to do. If we do not like working with difficult children, then perhaps we should think about finding another line of work.

# CHAPTER 5

---

# Changing Your Own Behavior

We have seen how people drive you crazy as a result of two factors: One has to do with their annoying, obstructive behavior, and the second is related more to your own attitudes and actions. Most often, it is not an either-or proposition, as both factors play a role.

Whereas in the next chapter we look more specifically at things you can do on the outside—that is, interventions, strategies, and techniques to influence others' behavior—first we deal with things that you can do to change the ways you operate internally. The goal is to have at your disposal a number of options that allow you to change your own perceptions, attitudes, and interpretations of difficult situations. This means that whether the other person changes or not, you can still feel better about how you have handled things.

## Detachment Without Withdrawal

I mentioned previously that there are times when taking a step back from the situation is helpful in reducing your level of perceived personal threat. The hard part is doing this without appearing or feeling punitive: "Okay, forget it! You don't care about all I am trying to do to help you, so I will just leave you to suffer alone."

The object of this position is not to disengage but to create needed distance when you are overinvolved. It is important to monitor closely the type and intensity of your relationship with a challenging student. Adjust your distance and involvement to a level where you protect yourself from hurt but also maintain your caring and compassion.

There was one 10th-grade girl about whom I was spending an inordinate amount of time worrying. She was clearly depressed, almost mute in class. Although her schoolwork was acceptable, it was obvious she was suffering terribly.

Each overture to reach out to her was met with stony resistance. Not only wouldn't she respond to any of my attempts to connect with her, but each time I tried something, she would retreat further. Apparently, I was making matters worse. Yet the more unsuccessful I felt, the harder I tried, continuing to push her further away.

Fortunately, I caught myself (actually, a friend pointed this out to me) trying too hard, caring too much, pushing things too fast. I made myself back off, which was very difficult, because I felt like I was abandoning her. I didn't withdraw from her completely; I just stopped pressing her, and inside my head, I decided to just let her go. I had already referred her to another professional for help. All I could do at this point was to let her go at her own pace. I had to stop taking this so personally, as if I could and would save her.

Whether with withdrawn, depressed students or with those who more actively sabotage your classroom, you must make certain that you don't get sucked into their stuff. There is a huge difference between empathy and codependence, between compassion and overinvolvement. Especially in those situations in which you feel things getting out of control, it is extremely important to detach yourself emotionally from things so that you can think more clearly and operate more effectively.

## Talking to Yourself

Mantras are used by meditators as a way to calm their breathing and maintain a sense of inner tranquillity. Usually, you repeat a mantra (a single word or syllable) to yourself over and over again to distract you from intrusions and to focus your concentration on the single task of staying relaxed.

In a similar vein, there are longer mantras that can be used during times of stress, especially in those situations where you find yourself locking horns with an obstinate student. The following are some helpful examples:

*"This isn't personal. This isn't personal. This isn't . . . ."* In other words, this saying is a reminder that students are not trying to get you personally (although it sometimes feels that way) but are merely trying to help themselves in the only way they know.

*"She is doing the best she can. She is doing the best . . . ."* If this child knew how to do anything else other than what she is doing, she would do it. She is trying to get along as best as she can in a world that has not provided her with many options. She is acting this way because it has worked for her before in the past. Just because you do not like it doesn't mean she must immediately stop.

*"In 100 years this won't matter. In 100 years . . . ."* In other words, this is a reminder to keep your perspective on things. What you are so upset about now is partially the result of blowing things out of proportion. This particular skirmish is an insignificant part of your day and life. It does not pollute the other positive things you are doing. It is only a minor annoyance and inconvenience, hardly a catastrophe. In 100 years, not only will you no longer remember or care about this particular incident, but neither will anyone else.

*"Think like an anthropologist. Think . . . ."* This is a reminder to apply what you know about cultural differences. Take a deep breath and a step back, and try to look at this situation more objectively. How is what the student doing a reflection of his or her cultural learnings?

This is but a sampling of possibilities. Each of them is intended to help you to calm down, take a step back, and remain in control. You have likely developed a few mantras of your own that help you during times of stress.

# Processing
# Disappointments Internally

Just as you can remind yourself to stay calm, cool, and collected in the face of adversity, you can also talk to yourself constructively and analytically. This helps you not only to remain in control but also to figure out what is going on.

Essentially, you adopt a rather objective, scientific stance to things, as if you are an outside consultant who is hired to make sense of the situation and make recommendations. You take on the detached position described earlier and ask yourself a series of systematic questions. It even helps to write down your responses in a journal:

*What are the signs that what you are doing isn't working?* What evidence is available to determine the specific effects of your efforts thus far? As objectively and dispassionately as you can, pay attention to the outcomes. You might document, for example, that a particular student has been getting better in his compliance to direct requests but shows little improvement in self-initiated tasks. Furthermore, you notice marked deterioration in cooperation with peers.

*What secondary gains is the student celebrating as a result of the failure?* Earlier, we looked at the "payoffs" people enjoy as a result of remaining stuck or dysfunctional. Remind yourself of which ones apply in this situation. Perhaps the student is enjoying a degree of power and control. Another common theme might be related to seeking attention. You will find that just looking at things in this way makes the behavior more comprehensible, less personally driven. You realize that the person is acting this way for a very good reason.

*What interventions have been most and least helpful?* Take inventory of what has worked well for you and what hasn't been so effective. We often get in trouble because we persist in doing things that are clearly not helpful, yet because they have worked before for us, we keep doing them anyway. Several steps are often helpful in this process:

1. Make a list of at least six things you have tried with a student that have not worked well.

2. Circle those items that you have tried multiple times without success.

3. Promise yourself not to do those things anymore that clearly do not work.

4. Brainstorm a list of at least six other things you could try instead of what you are already doing.

*Who has an interest in sabotaging your work?* Sometimes your efforts fail because someone behind the scenes has a strong negative influence. Perhaps peers or best friends are whispering in the student's ear, urging him or her to cause more trouble. Maybe there are things going on at home that are so dysfunctional that they undo any of your efforts. Maybe even another staff member is counteracting your attempts to be helpful.

In many cases, you might not be able to neutralize these toxic influences, but it is at least helpful to know what you are up against. Remember that you are only with kids a few minutes or hours per day compared to how much time they spend with friends and family. Knowing this, you can sometimes try to enlist the support of significant others to help you with goals.

*What in you is getting in the way of being more effective?* Look at yourself as well. In what ways have you lost your compassion and caring for this child? Granted, he or she is doing some things that make it very difficult to feel very loving toward him or her, but what is going on inside of you that is being obstructive? As best you can, try to own your contributions to the difficulty. Examine your own issues that have arisen as a result of this conflict. Explore other personal things going on in your life that might also be intrusive or part of the picture. It is likely, for instance, that if you are experiencing trouble in any of your other relationships—with family, friends, colleagues, or a partner—this will likely "bleed" over into your work with kids.

*What can you learn from this to help you grow?* One way to look at people who drive you crazy is that they were put in your life for a good reason. They can teach you things about yourself, and about the world, that you can't learn any other way. Sure, you'd prefer not to have to deal with such painful lessons, but there are still opportunities for you to grow a lot as a result of these encounters. In order for this to happen, however, you must be open to the possibilities that can emerge from these situations. You must remember to focus not only on the negative, painful, and annoying aspects of the relationship but also on what can be gained as a result.

*What outside resources can you tap?* One of the things that makes conflicted situations so challenging is that you feel so alone. On the other hand, you can go to trusted friends and colleagues to dump your troubles, but you will only feel worse as a result. That is why you must have good mentors, trusted confidants, and supervisors whom you can go to for help to talk things through. In some cases, this might be another teacher. Another excellent resource might be a school counselor. If you are lucky, one of the school administrators can help. If all else fails, it is sometimes a good idea to consult your own counselor for help.

Regardless of whom you go to for help, whether a family member, friend, colleague, or professional counselor, you must not carry the burden alone.

## Stop Complaining

I referred earlier to how counterproductive it can be to hang out in the teachers' lounge with those who are disenfranchised. Sitting around complaining and whining about how awful students are and how they don't care will win you sympathy for a minute or two; after that, you will just continue to feel like a victim. In addition, complaining to family and friends about how tough you've got it only continues to reinforce the idea that students are trying to make your life miserable. That is ridiculous; they are only trying to amuse and protect themselves.

Rather than complaining about your challenging students, try an experiment: Pick out one or two positive features about them and make it a point to discuss *those* qualities with colleagues and friends. Talk about how inventive the troublesome child is as an entertainer, what good aim he has in launching projectiles, what a beautiful smile he has, how quick he is at making friends. Such an exercise helps you to balance your annoyance with an appreciation for his strengths.

## Keeping Your Sense of Humor

There is no excuse for the line: "I just don't know why kids act the way they do." Sure you do. Because it is fun. If you were to step back and not take their behavior personally, you would recognize as comical the lengths to which some students will go to entertain themselves. One teacher keeps a catalog of all the antics she sees displayed in her classes. When someone comes up with an inventive variation of a new sound, projectile, or method of resistance, she actually feels excited at the prospect of recording it in her journal.

Of course, we cannot laugh out loud as often as we would like when we see students doing the weird and funny things they do. That is not to say, however, that we can't appreciate the creativity and humor of the gesture. Such a posture lightens things up considerably, reminding us that often this is a game, and not one to be taken all that seriously compared with the things that really matter.

## Reframing Problems

Sometimes you get in trouble because you are looking at the situation in a way that reinforces helplessness. If, for instance, a child is seen as "shy," there's little you can do about that. You have described a chronic, consistent pattern that is impervious to change. In fact, nobody behaves shyly in *all* situations. Look for exceptions. Reframe the problem so that it does not sound like, "You are shy," but rather, "You *act* shy in certain situations that are new for you, but once you start to feel comfortable, you demonstrate a range of behaviors."

Your goal is to figure out a way to define the problem so that you can more easily promote changes. Instead of thinking of students according to a label (learning disabled, attention deficit disordered, emotionally disturbed, fidgety, hostile), it is often helpful instead to describe specific behaviors that can be changed.

For example, the very idea of "disobedience" is discouraging. The implications are that this student is defying *you* and that now you must do something to ensure compliance. Instead, disobedience can be reframed as a form of "creative cooperation." This student is co-operating with you but simply in an unusual way. Such a redefinition of the problem suggests a different set of solutions.

Katrina was constantly drawing attention to herself in class. She was a master of animal sounds. Even more impressive, she could mimic bird calls without seeming to move her lips, so it was very difficult to catch her in the act.

The teacher attempted to restrain this "disruptive behavior" in every way he could imagine, all to no avail. During a moment of inspiration, he decided to reframe this behavior not as "challenging" or "disruptive" but as "clownish." This young student was simply being a clown, a court jester. Henceforth, the teacher was able to smile as a first reaction to her "Bawdy Parrot" (one of her best) rather than feeling challenged and enraged. Within the culture of her family, he knew that this was the way Katrina had always been able to distract her father and keep him from hurting her during his drunken bouts. In the culture of her peers, he realized that she en-joyed tremendous status because of her unusual talents.

The teacher called Katrina in for a conference, telling her that he greatly admired her skills as a clown. He then suggested, however, that she was performing for the wrong audience, because surely they did not give her the full attention she deserved. He offered to set aside some special class time to have her demonstrate her various comic skills; he figured that perhaps she would then no longer need to mimic birds during work time in class.

The point is not whether this particular suggestion worked with the student or not. Whether she changed her behavior in accordance with the reframe was less important than the teacher's being able to view her behavior as less threatening and more amusing. He was far more likely to discover some way to curtail her behavior, or at least to harness it, now that he was less emotionally agitated.

## Being Flexible

One of the most amazing things about teachers' attempts at discipline is that when we do something that doesn't work very well the first time, we persist in doing it again and again.

You yell at a child to stop punching a student in the seat next to him, yet he continues to do so. What do you do? Yell louder.

You punish a child by taking away some privilege, but it has no discernible effect. So what do you do? Take away *another* privilege.

You censure a student for talking out of turn, and what does she do? She becomes even more belligerent. So what do you do? Censure her again.

The simplest solution to sorting out any conflict is to figure out what you are doing that is not working—and don't do that anymore. Do something else—*anything* other than what you are already doing.

Noel is a restless, hyperactive 11-year-old who has been giving his teachers fits throughout the year. He does not sit still for more than a few minutes at a time and always seems to be in the middle of some sort of scuffle. Medication has been ruled out as an option, and the family is not open to counseling. The message has been clearly communicated: He's *your* problem, so you deal with him.

The teacher first made a list of all the things she had tried so far (repeatedly) with the boy that had not proven successful:

1. Gentle censures

2. Yelling at him to stop his disruptive behavior

3. Reminders that he is off task

4. Time-outs

5. Moving his seat

6. Distracting him with activities

7. Sending him to the office

The list goes on a bit longer, but you get the drift. The teacher has been engaging in her usual dozen interventions, none of which has worked very well. Like most of us, the teacher tries something: "Would you please stop making that noise?" Then, when he continues, she says again, "I told you to stop making that noise! Now if you do that one more time. . . ." The threat is left unsaid, because she realizes how futile it is to offer a prospective punishment because nothing works for this boy.

To be more accurate, the dozen strategies the teacher has tried over and over and over again do not work, but because she is stuck doing those same things, she can't create, devise, or invent something else. At this point we have no idea what would work with this young man, but we clearly know what will *not* work with him. Until the teacher stops doing those ineffective things, she will remain stuck. Yet once she agrees to stop doing what is most familiar, she can experiment with other possibilities and combinations that might prove more useful.

The hardest thing about this is that there are certain interventions, strategies, and things we say and do with which we are most comfortable. We do not like to give them up, even when they are not working. If you nag a child to do something and this has no impact on changing her behavior, rather than continuing to nag it is time to try something else. Although you may not know what will work, you assuredly know what will *not* work. You do not have to try that anymore and can devote your energies to experimenting until you find the right combination.

## Help Yourself First

Before you can ever hope to neutralize those students who drive you crazy, you must first take care of yourself. This means owning your contributions to the conflict. It means taking things less seriously and seeing the humor in many situations. It means keeping yourself calm in the face of adversity. It means thinking through things logically and analytically. It means getting help when you need it. Most of all, it means modeling to students how important it is to be in charge of yourself before you ever hope to influence others in a positive way.

# CHAPTER 6

# Strategies for Changing Students' Behavior

Before any intervention, discipline strategy, or helping skill is likely to be helpful, you must first be engaged with the student in such a way that you both feel respected and heard. No student is going to feel grateful for or responsive to finger-pointing in which you attempt to blame him or her for your discomfort with his or her behavior.

In this chapter I offer some specific suggestions as to what you can do during those times when you are at an impasse with a particular student—when your favorite strategies are not working and you feel at a loss about where to go next.

## Some Rules of Engagement

In the interest of resolving disputes with children you find challenging, several suggestions are offered. All of them are intended to be tried within the context of a constructive relationship that is built upon the solid foundation of trust, safety, and respect. Remember, too, that the ideal relationship will continually change according to the particular needs of the child and where you are in the process.

Consider, for example, the needy child. This is someone who wants more than you can give, usually to make up for long-term neglect or abuse suffered throughout life. In working with developmentally deprived children, Willison and Masson (1990) found that most often school personnel adopt a parenting role in their attempts to provide the nurturance and support that has rarely been offered. Specifically, this means:

1. Demonstrating love and affection

2. Creating a trusting relationship through brief multiple contacts over time

3. Providing a solid "holding environment," one in which firm limits are in place and promised consequences are delivered consistently

4. Offering constructive feedback regarding ways the child could better meet his or her own needs, or at least ways to get needs met in more socially appropriate ways

5. Presenting the figure of a benign authority who is dependable

6. Serving as an advocate for the child in negotiations with others

7. Teaching the child coping skills that are not currently part of his or her repertoire

Of course, these guidelines could be applied to work with *any* student, regardless of whether he or she is especially needy or not. The same is true with any of these other rules of engagement.

When attempting to resolve difficulties with a student, it is a good idea to follow some simple guidelines when giving constructive feedback (see Box 6.1). MacGrath (1998) recommends that these steps be followed in order to depersonalize the situation for both participants and to work toward a suitable resolution.

Another, more structured, option is to use the "behavior support plan" devised by Ayres and Hedeen (1998) in order to specify a student's strengths, areas of difficulty, and appropriate strategies for

---

**Box 6.1** Guidelines for Giving Constructive Feedback

- Present feedback in a private setting to avoid embarassing the student.
- Separate the person from the behavior in your statements.
- Use "we" statements whenever possible to demonstrate shared responsibility.
- Make feedback as specific as possible, giving supportive examples.
- Invite the student to share what he or she needs.
- Follow up by disclosing what you need in this relationship.
- Participate in mutual problem solving.
- Declare (or, better yet, negotiate) consequences if there is no change.
- End on a positive note.

---

intervention (see Table 6.1 for an example). Often the very process of writing out what the problems are and what you can do to respond helps you to feel more empowered as well as loaded with options that you might use.

## Primacy of the Relationship

No strategy, method, intervention, or skill works in isolation. Anything you do occurs in the context of a relationship you develop with each of the students in your classroom. When you encounter someone who drives you crazy, in a sense, that is fairly strong evidence that the relationship is somehow impaired. Yet the challenge of working with difficult children is learning to love the unlovable (Marlowe, 1999).

The first and best way to look for solutions to difficulties is by examining ways that your relationships with problematic students might be improved. Sometimes this could be a matter of showing a bit more attention (or less). In other situations, you might try face-to-face talk. The key, however, isn't so much what you do, but *how* you do it.

**Table 6.1** Example of a Behavior Support Plan

| Student Strengths | Student Weaknesses | Difficult Behavior | Meaning of Behavior |
|---|---|---|---|
| • Good sense of humor<br>• Likes to be liked<br>• Excellent art and computer skills<br>• Athletic<br>• Verbally expressive | • Poor impulse control<br>• Weak reading skills<br>• Little support at home<br>• Few friends<br>• Self-conscious about small size | • Temper tantrums<br>• Starts fights<br>• Demands excessive attention<br>• Gives up easily<br>• Doesn't turn in work | • Socially unskilled<br>• Emotionally immature<br>• Lack of support<br>• Enjoys failing on own terms<br>• Poor body image<br>• Possible learning disability |
| **Needed Skills** | **Prevention Strategies** | **Intervention Strategies** | **Strategic Responses** |
| • Improve reading<br>• Learn more socially appropriate skills<br>• Manage temper<br>• Learn alternative problem-solving skills<br>• Build on art and computer skills to expand interests<br>• Improve frustration tolerance | • Refer for assessment of learning disability<br>• Refer to counselor for anger control<br>• Recruit support of parents<br>• Change seating<br>• Allow child to show off strengths<br>• Build in opportunities for success | • Schedule brief interactions to improve relationship<br>• Negotiate limits<br>• Contract for homework<br>• Offer more positive attention<br>• Extinguish negative attention<br>• Privately confront and challenge his angry outbursts | • Schedule time-outs immediately after outbursts<br>• Reward child more often<br>• Don't let child get to me; remember this is a game to this child<br>• Give child more choices<br>• Laugh with child more often<br>• Reflect child's anger before it gets out of control |

Adapted from Ayres and Hedeen (1998).

Compare, for instance, the way two different teachers approach a child who has been a behavior problem in class.

Teacher 1: Karyn, you have been getting in trouble a lot lately. There was that situation yesterday with the fight. And then again today you couldn't seem to sit still. What's the problem with all this? Are you having some problem you want to tell me about?

This teacher is doing his best to show caring and compassion while working on a relationship with a student who has been driving him crazy. But what did you notice about the way he conducted this conversation?

Several things stand out:

1. He started out by putting the student on the defensive.

2. He focused on "you," on what the student was doing.

3. He asked interrogation-type questions ("What's the problem with all this?").

4. He asked "closed" questions (those that can be answered with "yes" or "no": "Are you having some problem you want to tell me about?").

Most likely, this student is not going to confide in the teacher under these circumstances, and the relationship is not going to be significantly improved. It is even possible that things could be made worse if the student believes she is being picked on, scolded, or censured.

In the second example, the teacher tries a different approach:

Teacher 2: I've been thinking about you a lot lately, feeling bad because I haven't been all that helpful to you. There is something I've been doing that has been irritating you, and I'd like us to sort out what we can do together to make things better. I think we're both upset and frustrated with one another lately. I'd really like it if we could figure out some way to make our relationship better.

Notice in this instance that the teacher uses the pronoun *we*, identifying the problem as a shared phenomenon. Rather than placing blame on the child or interrogating her, the teacher instead shares her concern in such a way that she owns her own contributions to the difficulties. At this point, she isn't worried as much about solving the problem or fixing the child's behavior as much as she just wants to build the beginnings of a better relationship.

There are some children, of course, with whom such a direct, trusting approach would never work; in fact, you'd get eaten alive if you admitted that a student is really getting to you. The point is not that you should always imitate this particular approach but that before you try any intervention, you should first work on strengthening your relationship as best you can.

## Improve Communication

So often, difficult interactions with children represent miscommunications in which both parties feel misunderstood and disrespected. The ones who particularly drive you crazy have probably not learned appropriate ways to express themselves. They may be emotionally immature and socially inept. We have also seen that many of them are also flooded with rage and resentment.

Without singling out any one individual in your class, you can spend time teaching students to be better communicators. This is a large part of what we do anyway, but it is especially relevant for angry students. Skramstad (1998) finds that her main strategy with resistant youth is to reach them through writing designed to help them find their voices.

If a person is driving you crazy, it's a good bet that he or she is making life difficult for others as well. Sometimes, this is a matter of being unable to find a place—in school, in the classroom, or in life—that feels okay. It may very well be a problem of "belongingness," in which our main goal is to help create a space that feels comfortable (Ellis, Hart, & Small-McGinley, 1998). If this can't be done within traditional classroom structures, then cooperative learning and peer-mediated assignments present viable alternatives (Taylor & Larson, 1998). In this way, you as the authority figure are not solely responsible for enforcing rules and blocking inappropriate behavior. This doesn't so much let you off the hook (okay, it does) as it exerts social pressure on troubled kids to conform to established norms that everyone else values.

## Use Counseling Skills

In other books (Kottler, 2000; Kottler & Kottler, 2000), I have talked extensively about the ways that teachers and administrators can use counseling skills in their work, even during brief, limited interactions. The essence of this approach involves practicing "active listening" skills, by which you demonstrate clearly and consistently that you hear and understand what a student is experiencing and respond appropriately to encourage deeper exploration of the problems.

Even during rushed 5-minute conversations, such skills can be applied to situations. In the following example, Nadine is obviously upset about her grade on her last assignment. Her face seems to be juggling two very intense emotions—anger toward you and frustration with herself. In the following dialogue, notice the way the teacher resists the temptation to be defensive and instead keeps the focus on Nadine's feelings.

> Teacher: Nadine, I can see you are really upset about something. What's going on? *The teacher leads by acknowledging Nadine's feelings, then asking an "open-ended" question, one that can't be answered in one word.*

> Nadine: It's just that this is so unfair. [Nadine drops the paper on the desk.]

> Teacher: You're really upset and disappointed with the grade you got. *The beauty of this approach is that even if the feelings you've reflected are not accurate, the student will simply clarify further. This takes pressure off you to do it perfectly.*

> Nadine: Well, yeah. I mean, I worked so hard on this, and I did everything you said we should do, and I still got this crappy grade. My parents are going to be really upset.

> Teacher: You tried as hard as you could and did everything you thought was required, but you still aren't happy with the result.

*This is a fairly superficial response, but it buys the teacher time until she can figure out what to say about the pressure Nadine is feeling from her parents.*

Nadine: Wouldn't *you* be? I really needed an A to boost my average, and this is going to make it impossible to get my grade up. Do you think I could do some extra credit?

Teacher: So you had a lot riding on this assignment and were hoping that this one would turn things around. You're feeling a lot of pressure to please your parents as well as yourself. *Notice that the teacher resists the temptation to get into a problem-solving mode. Instead, she sticks with what she hears under the surface of what Nadine is saying.*

In a counseling mode, the object of the interaction is neither to solve the problem nor to wave a magic want and make things all better. The goal is simply to listen compassionately, to try and understand the student's experience, and to prove that you are with her by clarifying what you are hearing. This involves just a few of the basic counseling skills; there are other skills you can use to help students move from this exploration and understanding stage to an action orientation.

If you have an interest in learning more about how to use counseling skills to resolve conflicts with difficult students, you might consider getting additional training or consulting basic sources (see Evans, Hearn, Uhlemann, & Ivey, 2000; Johnson, 2000; King, 2001; Kottler, 2000; Young, 2001).

## Get a Partner

A helping relationship is a partnership, one in which success depends very much on how well the participants are functioning together. Just as couples seek marital counseling when they are not getting along or adversaries seek mediation when they have reached an impasse, one solution to an irreconcilable conflict is to recruit some assistance from an outside source—that is, to double the resources available.

I discovered this strategy in a counseling situation when a colleague who was going on vacation asked me to take a few of his cases while he was gone. He warned me that with a few students in particular he had reached the end of his resources, and he welcomed anything I could do to improve the situations. Not wanting to engage in any deep-level counseling that might conflict with the work my colleague was already doing, I instead concentrated my efforts on asking the students to consider ways they could work harder and more effectively with their counselor once he returned. To my surprise, the students were most forthcoming and honest: They disclosed all the things they did not like about their sessions and shared exactly what they thought their counselor could do differently that would help them to open up more. Furthermore, they gave me permission to pass the advice along to him.

A few days after my colleague returned, he called to tell me about the breakthroughs that occurred with the students I had seen. The simple act of seeing a mediator, a neutral party, made a tremendous difference in breaking through the impasse that he had been experiencing with these students. This gave me the idea to expand the strategy further.

I had been having difficulty with a student I was seeing in counseling, a surly adolescent who refused to talk in our sessions; he would just pick at his face, scowl menacingly at me, and occasionally grunt. After the third session, there was overt hostility between us. Each of us felt angry and resentful toward the other, determined to win this struggle. Even worse, we were stuck with one another. His parents had firmly proclaimed that he would stay in counseling with me for a minimum of 6 months, whether either one of us liked it or not.

On a lark, one day I invited one of my officemates to join us in a session. Mostly my intention was to show my colleague how offensive this young man was, but during a moment of inspiration I decided instead to introduce him by saying to my colleague, "Look, we need some help. We seem to be stuck. Neither one of us particularly wants to work with the other, but we do not have a lot of choice here. We have more sessions scheduled together, and neither of us is particularly looking forward to them. I wonder if there is something that you can do to help us work things out?"

The boy smirked at that, but I could see he agreed. Actually, he was shocked at the way I presented things—I didn't blame him for our problems but rather framed the conflict as a circumstance that seemed to be beyond our control. After this introduction, it didn't matter so much what my colleague did with us. Verbalizing the notion that we owned our problems together and definitely needed some help to sort things out created a necessary shift in our work together. When the "visiting counselor" asked us to identify the main problems, what each of us was doing to contribute to these conflicts, and what we could each do differently, we were well on our way to sorting things out. Ever since that time, I have seen a lot of benefits to inviting a mediator into sessions when an obvious impasse has been reached. Sometimes that consultant can even be a friend of the student, someone who is willing to act on his or her behalf.

Within your school, there are a number of people you could invite in as consultants—a counselor, an administrator, another teacher, a student mediator. One option is even to ask the student to nominate a confidante whom he or she particularly trusts—another teacher in the school or a friend. The goal here is to promote a breakthrough by involving other parties to help sort things out.

## Conducting Conferences

In order to find out more about what's going on with a challenging student, invite the family in for a conference (the more the merrier, or at least the more informative). You need not be a family therapist in order to gather information about the way the unit operates, perhaps reinforcing the child's difficult behavior.

Taffel (2001) recommends looking for things such as the following:

- Who talks to whom in what tone of voice?
- Who's got the power and who doesn't?
- Who listens and who doesn't?
- Who interrupts?

Your job, of course, is not to do any sort of intervention, but merely to understand more about the child's background. If you suspect things are going on that might be amenable to treatment, you can make a referral to a counselor or therapist. You are far more likely to influence the family to follow your recommendations if you have some sort of working relationship with them.

In any conference you lead, follow these basic rules:

1. Keep things under control and don't let them get out of hand.

2. Don't allow anyone to be treated disrespectfully (including you).

3. Collect the background information you need.

4. Find out how the child is different (or the same) at home.

5. Offer constructive and supportive feedback.

6. Look for exceptions to difficult behavior (when the student is cooperative).

7. Look for evidence of developmental disorders or learning disabilities that might be useful in making a referral.

It is much easier to be patient and compassionate toward a student who drives you crazy when you realize that the annoying behavior may result from temperament. Taffel (2001) makes the point that certain stable personality factors related to sensitivity, mood, adaptability, tenacity, and energy predispose some children to struggle in certain circumstances such as those found in a classroom. They have little control in these situations and may be subjected to stressors that elicit overreactions.

## Let Go

There are times when you can drive yourself crazy trying to fix someone who doesn't want to be fixed. In spite of how skilled and knowledgeable you are, how dedicated and motivated, there are limits to what you can do. If a student is bound and determined to act disruptively, for whatever reason, sometimes the best you can do is to minimize the damage to yourself and others for whom you are responsible. Sometimes it is better to do less, rather than more.

It is senseless to argue with someone who likes to fight. There is no way you can win a battle of wills when the other person has nothing to lose. There are times when the best thing you can do is simply to let go of your investment in the outcome, shrug your shoulders, and tell the student (and yourself) that now just doesn't seem to be the best time to offer help. Perhaps sometime in the future things might proceed more successfully.

## Strategic Interventions

In addition to the general rules of engagement, there are a number of other strategies that often prove useful when working with cases you find challenging. Combining the work of "brief" or "strategic" therapists (see Cade & O'Hanlon, 1994; de Shazer, 1991; Nardone & Watzlawick, 2001; O'Hanlon, 2000; Sells, Schiff, & Haley, 1998), a number of interventions are often useful in breaking down barriers.

Time is the teacher's greatest enemy; there is precious little of it available to take care of all the kids in your charge, plus complete all the necessary daily administrative tasks. It is obvious, therefore, that you must devise ways to intervene efficiently with students who are having difficulty and, when appropriate, to make referrals to other school personnel who are trained and equipped to deal with difficult kids.

As I have mentioned before, although it is beyond the scope of your training and job to actually engage in counseling with students, it is still useful to have some idea how brief therapy methods work so that you may adapt some of the ideas to the classroom. At some later time you may wish to consult other sources that describe this approach in greater detail (see Littrell, Malia, & Vanderwood, 1995; O'Hanlon, 2000; Sklare, 1997).

There are several unique assumptions to this approach:

1. The problem is the problem. In other words, treat the presenting symptoms rather than trying to figure out what the "real" underlying issue may be.

2. Make sure the identified problem is one that both the student and you agree is disturbing. It does little good to work on an issue unless both of you agree that such efforts are appropriate.

3. Difficult behavior results from what is called "circular causality." There are interactive effects implicit in any interpersonal struggle: One person sparks reactions in the other, which in turn elicits other responses.

4. Disturbing symptoms represent the child's attempt to solve the problem. All behavior is functional on some level. We are all doing the best we can with what we know how to do. Find out whom the child is helping or protecting as a result of acting out.

5. Difficult students are stuck. They do not see other alternatives that work as well as what they are already doing.

6. Adopt a cautious and respectful attitude. Maintain a "one-down" position in which you present yourself in the role of consultant rather than authority figure.

7. Focus on the future. Rather than dwelling on what has already taken place, or even what is going on in the present, concentrate efforts on what *can* be done in the future.

8. Move beyond blame. First, it is impossible to determine who is solely at fault. Second, assigning guilt does not do anything useful to resolve the difficulty.

9. Find out as much as you can about the context of the problem. When does it occur? Where does it occur? With whom does it occur? When does it *not* occur?

10. Look for exceptions. Normal counseling asks people to talk about their problems. Instead, try exploring those instances when the child is successful and doesn't engage in the disruptive behavior.

11. The child has the resources to solve the problem. Assume that given sufficient support, encouragement, and guidance, the child can resolve things to everyone's satisfaction.

12. Small steps lead to big changes. Start with relatively small steps in the right direction.

13. Stay *very* flexible. Observe the current pattern before attempting any intervention. Note carefully the effects of what you are doing. Repeat what works; do not repeat what doesn't.

14. If the child isn't motivated to resolve things, then work with someone else (parents, siblings, friend).

Most of these assumptions underlie the techniques described below for working with challenging students.

## The Miracle Question

This technique is a staple of many problem-solving therapists: The student is asked to imagine a time in the future when, by some miracle, the presenting problem has been resolved. "Think about what would be different. What would others notice? How would you feel?" And then, "How was the problem solved? What did you do?"

To give you some idea how a counselor would use this method, listen in on the following dialogue:

Counselor: Hey guy! What's been up with you?

Flynn: Nothin'. Same ol'.

Counselor: I understand you've been having some problems lately.

Flynn: Nah! Just a misunderstanding.

Counselor: A misunderstanding? Seven detentions in a semester?

Flynn: What's the use? Anything I do won't change anything.

Counselor: I wonder if that's true. What if I could wave a magic wand and make everything better? What would things be like?

Flynn: For one thing, everyone would be off my back. [Laughs]

Counselor: That *would* be a miracle, huh? What else?

Flynn: Well, I ... you know ... I guess I wouldn't get in trouble so much.

Counselor: That might be a nice change of pace. What else?

Flynn: I don't know. My parents would leave me alone. I'd be
getting good grades and stuff.

Counselor: Okay. That sounds like a pretty nice future. Now,
how did you make that happen?

At this point there is often some resistance, both because what
we are asking the child to do is difficult and because whatever answer
is provided is actually the "magical"/solution. The significance of
articulating this out loud is that the student is actually describing
exactly what he or she needs to do to get back on track. When the
boy in the previous dialogue looked into the future, telling what he
did to fix things, he described himself as someone who was responsible, in control, and perfectly capable of making good things
happen. With the counselor's guidance, the emphasis was placed not
on what the student's teachers, friends, and parents would do differently but rather on what the student would do more effectively.

You will not be very effective using these same techniques without considerable training, experience, and supervision, but this does
give you some idea of what a counselor can do to be helpful and how
a professional might operate to change a dysfunctional pattern and
instill hope for the future.

## When Things Are Going Right

The problem with difficult students is that they are locked into a
pattern in which everyone, including the students themselves, is
always focused on what they are doing wrong. The frequency and
intensity of the disruptive behavior are often exaggerated, as if the
problem behavior were always occurring. Yet even the most belligerent student is sometimes considerate, the most withdrawn student
occasionally initiates things, and the most thoughtless student is
known to be responsible when he or she perceives something to be
important.

Remember to focus on the times when the student is in control
and doing quite well:

Teacher: I notice that we only talk together when you get into
trouble. I'd be interested to hear about the times when you are
on top of things.

Karyn: Well, if you talk to my mother or my other teachers, they'll tell you I'm always in trouble for one thing or another.

Teacher: I know it sure feels that way. Perhaps they do notice you mostly when you are acting up. I know that's been true with me as well. What I wonder, though, is what you are like when you are cooperative. Like right now, for instance. I find you very easy to talk to. What are some other times when you are doing well?

The emphasis, of course, is on balancing the negative aspects with positive aspects of the student's behavior. By emphasizing what the student is capable of doing, the teacher is actually encouraging her to be more responsible.

## Shake Things Up

If little changes lead to bigger ones, then the strategy should be to find some way to make even slight alterations in the way the student behaves. This can involve changes in the following:

- Rate of behavior—getting the child to repeat a behavior less often or, if that isn't possible, then *more* often initially (a change in *any* direction proves that the behavior is controllable)
- Duration of behavior—decreasing or increasing the length of time in which a child does something
- Intensity of behavior—encouraging the child to do something "softer" or "harder"
- Sequence of behavior—mixing up the order in which behaviors occur
- Location of behavior—changing the place or time of day in which the behavior occurs

By making any of these small changes, the child is demonstrating his or her capability to alter the way things are done. If we accept the systemic view that the problematic child is part of a larger interactive pattern, then even small changes in the student's behavior can spark more dramatic ones in others' behavior.

# Resolving Conflicts

Difficult behavior can be viewed from different viewpoints. Nobody sees him- or herself as the problem. Each person believes him- or herself to be perfectly reasonable and accommodating—it is the other person who is the problem. You have at your disposal several strategies that help troubled students to accept responsibility for their own behavior and make needed changes.

## Challenge Thinking

Another lesson borrowed from the arena of counseling is related to "cognitive therapy," a method that helps people to recognize self-defeating ways they talk to themselves and to substitute alternative self-talk. Developed by theorists Albert Ellis (1996) and Aaron Beck (see Beck & Freeman, 1990), this approach teaches students to identify their most consistently irrational beliefs and then challenge them with logical thinking processes (see Blau & Ellis, 1998; McMullin, 1999; Neenan & Dryden, 1999; Philips & Watts, 2001; Wessler, Hankin, & Stern, 2001).

In the spirit of cognitively based therapies, it is critical to help many children to think differently about their predicaments. The unmotivated student, for example, is often engaging in negative self-talk such as the following:

"I suck as a student."

"It'll never be any different."

"My teachers don't like me."

"I don't care about this stuff anyway."

These self-defeating beliefs must be challenged along the lines of finding the evidence to support them. Ideally, in group settings, Campbell (1991) suggests encouraging unmotivated students to confront one another. First of all, students must learn to differentiate those times when they are passionately driven to do something from those times at school when they are not. Next, they are encouraged to confront their negative messages with alternatives:

"I could be better as a student if I really tried."

"*Some* teachers don't like the way I *act.*"

"I'm afraid to care about school in case I can't succeed the way I want to."

In addition to this cognitive restructuring, Lewis (1992) stresses the role of helping children discriminate between those times when they do well and those times when they do not feel motivated:

- "Talk about that time in art class when your painting was displayed in front of the class. How did you manage that?"
- "What happened during social studies when you stopped trying? Without blaming anyone else, what happened inside of *you*?"
- "How do you account for the fact that other children do well in those situations? What's the difference?"
- "How do you explain that your times are so fast in the 50-meter race but your performance in math is so poor?"

In each case, we are helping the student to search for the internal self-perceptions that sustain negative beliefs about their capabilities. Lewis (1992) suggests that instead of waiting until children become unmotivated and blame others for their own lack of interest, we should be helping to prevent these problems through class activities. Such units could include structured explorations into what generates interest in school activities. Rather than blaming teachers for being boring (the most typical excuse), children are helped to develop ways they can make their own learning more dynamic. We can all think of times when other people were bored or disengaged but we weren't because of things we were doing differently. That lesson in self-responsibility can go a long way in taking the focus off others and helping students to reclaim their own responsibility.

## Applications to Oneself

One of the interesting strengths of a cognitive approach is that it works equally well when teachers apply the methods to themselves. This means that during those times and situations when you feel upset about something, you can change those negative feelings by altering your thinking and the ways you interpret the situation.

Imagine, for instance, that a student who drives you crazy is acting up in her usual ways. You are standing in front of the room, fuming inside, about to explode. If we could get inside your head and listen to the inner dialogue taking place there, we might hear statements such as the following:

1. "How dare this girl do this *to me!*"

2. "This sort of thing *always* happens to me."

3. "This is *awful* that I have to deal with these situations."

4. "I'm a lousy teacher *because* I can't handle this well."

5. "*This isn't fair* that I have to deal with this sort of stuff."

Each of these statements is in some way irrational or illogical or represents an exaggeration of reality. You can find the clues in the italicized words of each statement.

According to this approach, the reason you would be upset is not because of what the student is doing, but rather what you are doing to yourself: how you are choosing to interpret what is happening. If you tell these things to yourself, you will surely be upset. Every time. But if, on the other hand, you challenge these statements and hold them up to objective scrutiny, you might select alternative ways of thinking that would produce very different reactions in you.

If we review each of those statements in sequence, the internal dialogue that takes place inside this teacher might sound something like this:

1. This girl is *not* doing this *to me*. This isn't about me at all; rather, it is about her own need for attention. As long as I persist in overpersonalizing this, I'm going to remain very upset.

2. It might sometimes seem as if this sort of thing always happens to me, but that is a gross exaggeration. In fact, I enjoy excellent relationships with many of my students. Now that I think about it, this is one of the very few kids who give me

trouble like this. Rather than this always happening to me, it is actually quite rare that it occurs, even with this one young lady.

3. This might be annoying, inconvenient, uncomfortable, and certainly undesirable, but it is hardly *awful,* which represents an extreme state. This is *only* mildly irritating. If I tell myself it's awful, then I'm going to be very upset. If, on the other hand, I remind myself that it is a small inconvenience, then I am not nearly as disturbed.

4. Just because I don't handle this one student as well as I would prefer does not make me a lousy teacher, only a human one. I am fallible and imperfect. This is just one of those times that I am not at my absolute best. This student is not driving me crazy; I am doing that to myself.

5. The world is clearly not fair. If things were really all that equitable, then I wouldn't have to deal with annoying, unmotivated students in the first place. But such is life. I can whine and complain about things, or I can just accept those aspects of this job that I can do little to change.

Obviously, such self-talk takes a lot of practice, considering you have had years of experience distorting and exaggerating situations, thinking irrationally and illogically, and blowing things way out of proportion.

## Applications to Other Situations

We started out in the previous chapter looking at ways to prepare yourself mentally and emotionally for coping with students who drive you crazy. In this chapter, we examined things that you can actually *do* to influence disruptive students' behavior. If these strategies work just as well with yourself as they do with your students, then perhaps you will not be surprised to learn that they can be applied with equal effectiveness to *any* conflicted relationship. Because some coworkers or parents may drive you just as crazy as any of the kids you encounter, we turn next to the thorny problem of difficult colleagues.

# CHAPTER 7

# Parents and Colleagues Who Drive You Crazy

"**L**ook. It's not so much that I don't like the way you're handling things [*read: "I don't like the way you are handling things"*] as that I disagree with the policy that has been established. I have been your greatest advocate [*to your face—behind your back, I undermine you every chance I get*]. I really want you to be successful [*only to the extent that it makes me look good*]. You have to trust me [*Don't trust me*] if you expect me to help [*Help? I will make sure you fail with every resource at my disposal*]. It just pains me so to see you struggling [*pains me that I cannot see more*], and I want to run interference for you [*"interfere" is just about right*]. So now, tell me what is going on with you."

Under the cloak of sincerity and apparent good intentions lurks a deceptive, manipulative individual whom you can neither trust nor open up to without covering yourself against ambush. This may be an administrator to whom you report, the parent of one of your students, another teacher, or a secretary in your school. In any case, you are forced to interact with this person on a regular basis.

## The Least of Our Problems

Sometimes, uncooperative students are the least of our problems. It is, after all, children's primary job in life to test limits, entertain themselves as best they can, protect themselves from perceived assaults, and challenge adults whom they believe are acting unjustly. Conflict in such circumstances is inevitable.

We were duly warned in school that we would face students who would drive us crazy. We were told about discipline problems and about uncooperative parents. We were alerted to problems associated with substance abusers, victims of abuse, intractable diseases, chronic behavioral and emotional disorders, and the like. So, as much as we might complain about how students often give us a hard time, this circumstance hardly takes us by surprise.

What may come as a shock is the extent to which some of our most challenging struggles at work have little to do with the students we see—it is our colleagues who often make life difficult. The good news, however, is that the same concepts and strategies that work well with difficult students are equally effective with anyone else who drives you crazy.

## Teachers Who Don't Understand

You'd think that in a job as difficult as ours we would all be pitching in to help one another flourish, or at least survive. Burnout, stress disorders, and plain old demoralization are so common that we don't even seem to notice anymore. Teachers are leaving the profession at such a rapid rate that schools should have revolving doors.

With all the pressures we face, conflicts we encounter, and students who drive us crazy, we need all the support we can get. Unfortunately, we are often our own worst enemies. Teachers, counselors, and administrators are known to undermine one another's efforts. Just as in any human organization, there are petty arguments, political skirmishes, and struggles for power and control over resources. And there is more than a fair share of tension among staff members.

There are a number of very good reasons why conflict exists among staff members in any organization.

*There are arguments over ideology.* What is the best way to work with children? Such a debate might even be constructive, if it were really designed to teach rather than to be won. What often happens, unfortunately, is that one or more educators believe that they are right and that everyone who doesn't subscribe to the same beliefs is incompetent or dangerous. Under such circumstances, discussions about policies and procedures are really about struggles for power: Who will control what we do and how we do it?

There are a number of very important and legitimate disagreements among educators about such things as how time and resources should be allotted, which specialized programs should be implemented, who should take on which assigned roles, and even what primary direction things should be moving toward. These are certainly constructive debates—if they are conducted respectfully. And that is a big *if.*

*There is competition for opportunities and resources.* Teachers are often placed in a competitive situation in which there are relatively few opportunities for obtaining advancement, new resources, and the plum jobs. In some schools or districts, teachers feel compelled to make themselves look good at the expense of others.

*There are personality clashes.* Some people just don't get along very well with others. Actually, I am being polite. What I am really thinking about are those folks in our field who are scary. They became teachers in the first place because they liked to be in control over other people's lives. Over time, they began to take themselves *very* seriously, as if they were not only important but far brighter and more capable than anyone else. They saw teaching as a way to become trained in the skills of being manipulative and even more powerful. In a sense they were right: Teacher education does prepare us with the knowledge and skills to more effectively get others to do things they might not want to do.

These wayward colleagues, once they became teachers, developed even more rigid, self-centered, and manipulative patterns. Perhaps you've met or worked with someone like this before. They like to play mind games. They actually enjoy conflicts—these are the times they feel most alive. They are exquisitely sensitive to each person's weaknesses and vulnerabilities, and they feel no compunction about exploiting them every chance they get. Although you may have an agenda to work cooperatively with colleagues, these individuals thrive on petty squabbles, if not outright war. They like the feeling of power that comes with making other people feel as miserable as they do most of the time.

## Administrators Who Handcuff Us

Administrators can sometimes be the greatest source of conflict. They assign us tasks that have nothing to do with teaching children. They handcuff us with rules and regulations that make it nearly impossible for us to do our jobs. At times it seems like they've forgotten what it's like to be a teacher.

As but one example, your principal is very passive and avoids conflict at all costs, with anyone. He will not back you up during those times when you need support. He will not defend your efforts to initiate new programs in your school. He just doesn't like to make waves. When you go to him for assistance about some matter, he couldn't be more cooperative; the problem, however, is that he will not actually do anything to follow through on his promises.

As hard as you work to help the children in your school, you feel as though you are constantly hanging on a limb, one that at any moment will snap and send you crashing to the ground. You try to get the support and supervision you need elsewhere in the district, but within the school itself you feel very alone.

## Parents Who Fight Us

Parents are another breed altogether. Technically, they are our colleagues as well as the caretakers of our students. Theoretically, we should be coordinating our efforts, collaborating in constructive ways, and sharing information to make each of our jobs flow more smoothly. They should be doing all they can to make sure their children are respectful, well fed and cared for, and eager and motivated to do their work. Certainly, this is the case with many families. However, every semester there are a handful of parents with whom we must deal who amaze us with their vindictiveness, abusiveness, and lack of responsibility. They accuse us of being incompetent or misunderstanding their poor, unappreciated child. They scream at us for not complying with their advice. They bad-mouth us to our supervisors, and even to their own children, undercutting our authority and ability to make a difference. When all else fails, they may even threaten us with bodily harm.

Most parents are cooperative and eager to do what they can to aid our efforts. There are a few, however, we encounter every semester who certainly shed some light on why their kids are so difficult to handle. Although the following is hardly an exhaustive list, parents who drive us crazy come in several forms:

- The entitled parent fully expects that we have nothing else to do but cater to their particular needs.
- The hostile parent is aggressive and inappropriately angry.
- The overly protective parent believes his or her child can do no wrong and is never at fault.
- The manipulative parent has a hidden agenda that will never be shared.
- The addicted parent is out of control.
- The incompetent parent may mean well but doesn't have a clue about how to do his or her job.

Regardless of the parents you are dealing with, your job is essentially the same: to win their support and recruit their assistance. Admittedly, this may be especially challenging with those kinds of parents just described.

The first task is to find out what the parents really want: What is their goal? What is their agenda? Usually, this is a variation of the following themes:

- "I want you to agree that I'm right and this is not my fault."
- "I want you to tell me how smart/talented/creative my child is."
- "I want you to fix my child . . . and I want immediate results."
- "I want to use you as a scapegoat so I can blame you for everything that doesn't go the way I want."

You can't, or won't, do what is expected, of course, but it is an important starting point to know where you stand. During this beginning stage of a meeting, I hear the following messages all the time: (a) Listen to me and don't interrupt, (b) agree with me, (c) reassure me that I'm not the problem, and (d) fix the problem and don't bother me anymore.

Parents, like teachers, are often stuck doing the same things over and over again, but because it is familiar to them, they are reluctant to abandon the ineffective strategies. Imagine, for example, that you have an incorrigible 16-year-old girl who is not responding well at school or at home. You ask for a recent example of the girl's acting out.

"Well," the mother begins, "the other day she refused to do her chores—she doesn't have that many to do but I try to give her . . ."

"You were saying . . ." you interrupt, getting her back on track.

"Oh yeah. Sorry. I just get so frustrated, you know."

"Yes, as a matter of fact I do know, because I deal with her in class every day."

"So anyway, I went in her room and she told me to get the hell out." The mother looks right at you to see if you flinch at the use of the swear word. Because you remain unmoved, having heard such words many times before, she continues: "Those were her exact words. Can you believe that?"

"So, then what happened?"

"Well, I told her in no uncertain terms such tone and language would not be tolerated in our house."

You're sure that went over well. Right. "And then what did you do?" you ask, already pretty certain what she will say next.

"She pushed me out and slammed the door. Can you believe it?"

"And then what happened?"

"I yelled at her and told her that behavior would just not be tolerated."

"Yes?" you continue to probe.

"She crawled out the window of her room and stayed out all night. She came home at 9 the next morning. I have no idea where she'd been."

"So, what did you do then?"

"Well, then I *really* gave her a piece of my mind."

"What effect did that have?"

"She ran up to her room again and slammed the door."

There is a pattern here, of course, although the mother isn't exactly seeing it. We can be critical of this parent and how oblivious she is of how ineffective her methods are, but we sometimes do the same thing—remain stuck doing things that don't work.

Whether you are dealing with difficult or cooperative parents, you can be very helpful to them by guiding them to look at what isn't working and to try alternative strategies instead. This is especially important with parents who may be neglectful or emotionally abusive, an all-too-frequent situation that often results from a lack of appropriate parenting skills or from the situation of parents who just don't like their children (Iwaniec & Herbert, 1999).

## Strategic Interventions

In the field of counseling, one approach that is becoming increasingly popular because of its fast-acting interventions is called "strategic" (Madanes, 1981; Quick, 1996), "problem-solving" (O'Hanlon, 2000), or "solution-focused" (de Shazer, 1991) therapy. The basic method involves following a few simple rules:

1. Ask the student to do something in a straightforward way. If the student complies, then the strategy is effective, and you can use it again. "I'd like you to go sit down in your seat and begin the assignment."

2. If the student modifies the task in some way, then offer an easily changeable task that is ambiguous. That way, the student isn't actually disobeying, because the instructions are

deliberately vague. "I see you've chosen to do some creative drawing instead of the assigned work. I'd like you to keep working on the assignment."

3. If the student doesn't do what was asked, don't ask him or her to do that anymore. "Let's try something else instead."

4. If the student does the opposite of what was asked, then use a "paradoxical directive" in which you prescribe the symptom. "Everyone else continue with the assignment . . . except you, David. I'd like you to continue your drawing."

As you can tell, this strategic approach can be rather manipulative. Essentially, what you are doing is showing extreme flexibility and fluidity. When something doesn't work, you don't do that anymore but instead try something else. Rather than challenging or confronting behavior directly, you go with the flow, so to speak.

In any of these situations previously described, but especially with difficult parents, there are several strategies that often prove useful.

*The one-down position.* Adopting this posture means that you do not challenge parents directly but rather solicit their help in a respectful, even pleading way. This is sometimes difficult to do because it may mean that you will have to be deceptive in order to win their cooperation:

> Teacher: Mr. Buzzwell, you seem to know so much more about this situation than I ever could learn. And you obviously have a number of great ideas about what I could do to better help your daughter. I wonder if you might be willing to come in for a few minutes and set me straight about what is going on. I seem to have missed some very important things to which you have alluded. I'm really interested in hearing more.

This, of course, is a very effective way to reduce conflicts with difficult parents by not challenging their competence or authority. By adopting a one-down position, we are deferring to their expertise, an invitation that is most difficult to resist.

*How can I help you?* Similar to the previous strategy, this attitude presumes that the difficulty we are experiencing with a particular parent exists in part because of conflict over power and control. The parent is feeling threatened by us, perhaps even ashamed about things we might know about the family or their competence as care-takers of their children.

> Teacher: What I am trying to say, Mrs. Whitaker, and I'm not saying it very well, is that my job is to help you do your job better. I have it easy—I only deal with your child for a few hours per week, but you have to live with him. I'm wondering what I can do to help you.

There is an attitude implicit in this strategy that reminds us not to fight with parents who challenge our authority or competence. Things can quickly escalate into a yelling match, and in all such circumstances, it is the child who loses the most. We must do all we can to charm parents into working cooperatively with us.

*Introducing ideas.* There are a number of things that some parents don't understand about their children. Sometimes, we can circumvent difficulties by explaining concepts that may be new to some people:

- Testing authority is normal and helpful for children.
- Children do what they have learned works best.
- Your child is doing the best she can.
- This is not your fault.

During our efforts at parent education, it is this last idea that is often most helpful of all. If parents aren't blaming us or their kids, then they are likely blaming themselves. Our best strategy is to stop all attempts at finding fault and instead work together to find solutions.

## What About You?

Yes, I'm talking to *you!* It is easy to blame parents or colleagues for making our lives difficult, for sabotaging us, for making our jobs and lives far more difficult than they need to be. It is easy to point the finger at someone else—a neglectful principal, an ungrateful teacher, an abusive parent, or an incompetent colleague. If what I said earlier with respect to challenging children is true—that sometimes they don't come to us as difficult, but we make them that way—then the same thing is possible with many of our so-called difficult colleagues.

The question to ask yourself, one that you clearly will not like, is: What is *your* role in being obstructive with others? If you accept the premise that conflicts almost always result from the contributions of both parties, then you must look at what you are doing to create or exacerbate such arguments. In other words, if someone were to research systematically how you are perceived by those with whom you most often find yourself in disagreement, what would these individuals say about you?

It is highly likely that there are a number of things you say and do that consistently get you in trouble. These are patterns that have been present from your own childhood and that are probably quite familiar to you and the other people who have been on the receiving end of them. In fact, it might be profitable for you to consider these recurring conflicts that you have lived through again and again in slightly different forms.

What I am suggesting to you is that we are primarily the authors of our own life stories. Certainly, we must contend with other people who may be unscrupulous, unreasonable, or abusive, but these folks do not necessarily act this way with everyone—only those who either invite this behavior or ignite it through their actions.

As one example of this phenomenon, let me recount the story of a colleague who was giving me an awful time. He was undermining me every chance he got—bad-mouthing me to students, contradicting me behind my back, creating problems that I would have to solve, placing students in situations in which they would have to choose whether to be loyal to him or to me. In short, he did everything he could think of to make my life difficult. Furthermore, he was an easy target to blame, as he was unpleasant to others as well. This made my role as a victim even easier—I spent months feeling sorry for myself, recruiting support for my positions, and cataloging all the crazy things he was doing that I found inappropriate and unprofessional.

It got my attention, however, when I started realizing that there were indeed people around with whom he had solid, healthy relationships. So, I asked myself, what did I do to deserve his wrath? What was I doing to invite him to treat me so poorly? How was I aggravating him in ways that were coming back to haunt me?

In all honesty, I must admit that I did not like doing this one bit. In some ways, I enjoyed being a victim of his abuse—I must have, or I wouldn't have tolerated things for so long! I also liked commiserating with allies, friends, and families about the latest indignity that I suffered. In some ways, I am reluctant to admit, I also liked doing little things that I knew would irritate the heck out of him. On some perverse level, all of this was immensely entertaining.

Once I began looking at what my role was in this conflict, I was surprised at how my sense of powerlessness vanished. I no longer felt that he was doing something *to* me, as much as that we were doing some sort of weird dance together. Although this realization didn't offer me any clues as to how I could get him to treat me any differently, it did suggest some new ways that I could conceptualize the conflict. No longer would I blame him for acting like a jerk, because he clearly acted in that manner only with those people who interacted with him in certain ways.

Of course, this pattern was familiar to me in my life. I could recall others with whom I had been locked into similar dynamics. I hadn't been all that successful previously in working through these struggles, but this time I was determined to do things differently. I cannot say, in all honesty, that I ever did get this guy to stop his behavior completely. I tried setting limits. I experimented with various ways of responding to him. Nothing worked very well except what I did inside my own head: I stopped blaming him for doing the best he could. I eventually left this job, partially to get away from him. You probably aren't surprised to learn that he showed up again in a slightly altered form in every other job I have had since then. What I hope is different now, however, is that I am much more interested in looking at what I do to invite conflicts rather than at what other people do that I find so disagreeable.

There are limits, however, to the extent to which you can take responsibility for difficult relationships, especially when you are dealing with people who become abusive.

# Those Who Abuse You

*I DON'T CARE WHAT YOU THOUGHT I MEANT: I AM TELLING YOU RIGHT NOW WHAT I WANT—NO, WHAT I DEMAND THAT YOU DO. I WILL NOT QUIET DOWN AND I AM NOT OUT OF CONTROL. I am just trying to get through to you. You obviously have a hard time understanding even the most basic instructions, and it burns me that you do not listen. I am trying to be reasonable with you, but that is quite difficult with someone who is so deficient in as many areas as you are. That is why, you poor excuse for a teacher, I have to resort to being a little loud in order to get your attention.*

*HOW DARE YOU QUESTION MY MOTIVES! IF YOU WANT SOME TROUBLE, I'LL GIVE YOU MORE THAN YOU CAN HANDLE. Do we understand one another?*

People who are abusive almost cannot help themselves. Their violence, aggressiveness, unbridled anger, and lashing out at others result from poor impulse control. They believe very strongly that other people are at fault for almost everything. Blame is a way of life for these individuals:

- "If only you would have listened to me the first time, I would not have had to resort to such extreme measures."
- "If you would just do your job the way I asked you to do it, then I would not have to yell."
- "You made me so mad I had no choice but to teach you a lesson."
- "You should know better than to do that; you know what it does to me. Gee, I'm sorry I got a little carried away. Are you alright?"

There are times when other people in your life, whether they are staff members in your school, students, parents of your students, or your own family and friends, consistently create disturbances that draw you in. In spite of your best efforts to negotiate some sort of truce, the interactions with these people remain uncomfortable, even distasteful.

You do not feel respected, nor do you feel that the other person is all that interested in getting along.

In some cases, there is little that you can say or do that will change others' behavior. You can resort to guerilla warfare, join them in the slippery mud that they so enjoy wallowing in. You can remain in a victim role, allowing others to abuse and take advantage of you. You can feel sorry for yourself and experience many of the symptoms of depression, helplessness, and demoralization. You can leave the scene altogether, but that probably won't work either because you'll encounter someone else just like your nemesis in your very next job. You can run but you can't hide.

So, what *can* you do to deal with difficult colleagues? Like so much of what we have already covered in this book, most of the work takes place inside your own head and heart. The truth of the matter is that you have very little power and control to change others, especially if they are on a supposedly equal footing with you. There is some leverage at your disposal when you are dealing with students who are driving you crazy, but with colleagues, it is a different story altogether. Such individuals may be better positioned (and a lot more experienced) at intimidation. Furthermore, they may actually enjoy such battles.

There is a wonderful expression that is frequently heard in the field of substance abuse that warns people not to allow others "to live inside their heads rent free." What this means is that it is bad enough to have to put up with difficult, ornery people at work. But *you* are the one who invites them into your head after you leave. You have conversations with them inside your head when you are coming to or leaving work. You invite them into the shower when you relive the conflicts, even into your bed when you think about them at night! Even if you can't do a single thing to change their behavior or the ways they act toward you, assuredly you can kick them out of your head, especially since they are not paying you rent to live there!

In order to banish obsessive ruminations and the tendency to beat yourself up, you must first accept the reality that other people are allowed to be the way they are even though you might not like it. It would be a wonderful world indeed if everyone were just like you; embraced the same values; and behaved with the same degree of respect, politeness, and civility that you believe is important. It would also be nice if everyone got along beautifully and there were not conflicts. But obviously, this is not going to happen.

If you wish to survive and flourish in any human organization, you must develop coping strategies for dealing with people who drive you crazy. Recall that the title of this book is phrased in such a way to imply that other people are not intrinsically difficult; we often make them that way based on how we choose to deal with situations, both during our interactions and inside our own heads.

# CHAPTER 8

---

# Preventing
# Future Problems

$A$ mong the first contemporary researchers to investigate systematically the challenges teachers face with difficult students were Jacob Kounin and his associates (Kounin, 1970; Kounin, Friesen, & Norton, 1966). In naturalistic studies, Kounin and his collaborators observed the proceedings of classrooms that contained one or more emotionally disturbed children.

Perhaps today, with our understanding of systemic and cultural influences on behavior, it is not surprising that Kounin discovered an interactive effect between teacher and student co-actions. So-called difficult students were not disruptive in all their classes; much depended on what the teachers did and how they did it. In these landmark studies, Kounin found that when teachers kept momentum going at a constant, stimulating pace, students were less likely to act out. It also helped significantly when teachers initiated smooth transitions between subjects. Once the teachers recognized that interest was waning, attention was wandering, or confusion was developing, they moved on, thereby preventing discipline problems *before* they occurred.

Although this research was completed over 30 years ago, it is still an excellent reminder today. All too often, educators are prone to blame the student as the only problem while refusing to examine the roles and influences of other factors.

"Sure I was tough to deal with," one grown-up ex-troublemaker discloses, "but what do you expect? Some of my teachers were so clueless I had to do something to spice things up. Either that or die of boredom."

## Proactive Versus Reactive Strategies

The best way to deal with people who drive you crazy is to not let things get to the stage where you become so bothered that you lose control. After all, if a student, parent, or colleague has really gotten to you to the point where you spend a lot of time thinking and talking about them, then you are already in trouble. By far, the preferred strategy is to design your work (and your life) in such a way that you avoid severe conflicts before they get out of hand.

Although some of the prevention strategies discussed apply only to your work in schools, most of the concepts can be applied to the way you conduct your life in general. If you wait until the point that you are already encountering trouble, you are far more likely to respond to the situation impulsively rather than reflectively. One model for dealing with students who drive you crazy is to first identify their primary needs (Canter & Canter, 1993). In other words, what are they looking for (see Table 8.1)?

Some students are acting out because they lack focus and direction, others because they have problems with motivation, still others because they want more attention or firmer limits. Until you can assess accurately what each of your challenging students is looking for, you are going to be hard pressed to neutralize their behavior.

Once you know what a student wants, you can then find alternative ways to meet those needs. The hard part, of course, is using empathy to get inside the student's skin, imagining what it must be like to be him or her. This is particularly challenging to do with students with whom you are already embroiled in conflict.

If one part of preventing problems is being more attentive and observant about what students need, the other part is being less reactive

**Table 8.1**  Needs of Difficult Students

| Observable Behavior | Primary Needs |
|---|---|
| Out of control | Asking for limits |
| Act bored | Want to be entertained |
| Feel disrespected | Want revenge |
| Feel threatened | Search for self-protection |
| Lack interest | Need motivation |
| Feel powerless | Want control |
| Feel stupid | Want validation |

Adapted from Canter and Canter (1993).

and more proactive. Being reactive means simply responding to what occurs, without the time available to plan strategic interventions. Responding proactively, on the other hand, allows for reflective action and avoids impulsive actions.

In Table 8.2 are examples of ways that reactive interventions can be changed to more proactive strategies. For instance, in the first one, instead of saying to yourself, "Why is she doing this to me?" you might instead depersonalize the situation by reminding yourself, "This isn't about me."

In any given situation in which you find yourself, you always have a choice about the ways you can respond, both internally and externally. The only way you can demonstrate this kind of mastery and control, however, is by thinking through situations *before* they occur.

**Table 8.2**  Changing Reactive Behaviors

| Reactive Intervention | Proactive Intervention |
|---|---|
| Overpersonalize behavior | Depersonalize behavior |
| Become emotionally activated | Remain calm and in control |
| Try to change student's behavior | Change how you respond |
| Respond automatically | Select response from options |
| Use generic, standard methods | Individualize intervention |
| Communicate frustration | Communicate caring |

Gootman (2001) distinguishes between two different kinds of interventions after a student misbehaves. "Low-key discipline" includes signaling, reminding, warning, ignoring, and praising. These subtle, strategic behaviors are far more desirable (for everyone) than "discipline with a capital D." Because in this book we are talking about those students who are already driving you crazy, it is likely that the milder forms have already failed.

As was suggested earlier, you must find the reasons for the student's behavior before you can hope to respond effectively. What are the triggers? What are the benefits to the student? What are your contributions to the problem?

Among other suggestions, Gootman (2001) advocates the use of consequences rather than punishments for misbehavior. If a student writes on his desk, for example, the *punishment* would be to send him to the office; the *consequence* would be for him to clean his desk.

Table 8.3 summarizes Gootman's (2001) ideas on why difficult students misbehave and what you can do about it. There are no real surprises in this table. Basically, most of the preferred interventions come down to communicating clear expectations, teaching children to be responsible for their actions, enforcing limits and rules consistently, and keeping yourself under control. The last condition can only be met when you develop the capacity to respond to annoying situations with relative objectivity and tranquillity. By definition, if a student is driving you crazy, that means you have lost your sense of balance.

## *Paying Attention to Feedback*

Often students become ornery and act out because they aren't motivated to learn or even to cooperate (Burden, 2000). Teachers are not motivated themselves to find out what truly interests these "difficult" children. In one sense, their disruptive behavior can be viewed as clear, direct, and consistent feedback that what you are doing is not working for them. They are telling you, over and over again, in the most dramatic ways possible, that you are not meeting their needs.

There are a number of possibilities for why this might be the case. Most obviously, such students might have expectations that you (or

**Table 8.3** Proactive Interventions With Misbehavior

| Misbehavior | Reasons for Misbehavior | Interventions |
|---|---|---|
| Breaks rules, interrupts | Ignorance, inexperience | State expectations more clearly, provide practice for desired behavior |
| Fidgeting, restlessness | Physical immaturity, boredom, attention problem | Adjust expectations, provide more realistic tasks |
| Silliness, talking out of turn | Emotional immaturity | Guide appropriate behavior, adjust expectations |
| Breaks things, touches everything, experiments | Curiosity | Require consequences, allow free time for experimentation |
| Defiant, aggressive, manipulative | Need for belonging, conduct disorder | Limit setting, cooperative learning opportunities |
| Clowning | Need for attention | Teach responsibility, validate when possible |
| Provocative behavior, tantrums | Need for power and control, impulse disorder | Set limits, enforce consequences |
| Verbal and physical aggression | Anger, control | Teach consequences, set limits, anger control |
| Teasing, irritating behavior | Adventure, fun, enjoyment | Awareness, problem solving, consequences |
| Lies, steals, cheats | Fear | Listening, problem solving, responsibility |

Adapted from Gootman (2001).

anyone) can never meet. Other possibilities directly related to the teacher's planning that are worthy of consideration include the following:

1. The lessons are not challenging enough and students become bored.

2. The material presented is beyond what students can handle, so they give up.

3. The lessons are not relevant to students' interests, so they disengage.

4. The presentation is so disorganized that the students can't track what is going on.

5. Students don't believe the teacher likes, respects, and cares for them.

One sure way to prevent, or at least minimize, acting out by difficult students is to consider what you are doing (or not doing) that might be aggravating or triggering their misbehavior. It is all too easy for us to look at their actions without considering our own contributions.

## Teacher Strategies
## That Maintain Momentum

It is when you are feeling weak and vulnerable that you are most prone to being unduly bothered by the actions of others. On good days, you can laugh at the feeble (or determined) efforts of others who are trying to drive you crazy. When you are operating at peak efficiency, nothing or nobody can really upset you for very long.

1. *Have realistic expectations.* One way to get yourself in trouble is to hold expectations for others that they can never meet.

2. *Push yourself to take risks.* When you become stale, when your life takes on too many predictable routines, you lose

much of your excitement for what you are doing. Make a commitment to continually change what you do and how you do it. This applies not just to how you teach but also to how you live your life. Become a model for your students of someone who is fearless and courageous in venturing into unknown territory.

3. *Take victories where you can get them.* Rather than focusing on your failures and disappointments, celebrate even modest successes. Pay attention less to those who drive you crazy and much more to those with whom you enjoy good relationships.

4. *Find the best in people.* Even those who give you the most trouble still have redeeming qualities. Look not only at what they do that you find annoying but also at what they have to offer.

5. *Don't work harder than the students.* This is a reminder to accept the limits of what you can do. Your job is to provide the best possible environment that makes learning possible, but you can't teach anyone who really doesn't want to learn. This is frustrating, but it is the reality of the way the world works.

6. *It's relationships, not content, that matter most.* Don't get too carried away with the idea that learning is only about mastering ideas, filling up students with stuff. If you think back on what mattered most to you in school, you'll remember that the teachers who were most influential were those you liked and respected the most.

7. *Keep a sense of humor.* Teaching can be a grim business. You face a lot of challenging situations every day and also some pretty annoying individuals. Try not to take things so seriously. Try not to overpersonalize situations.

8. *Learn to metabolize stress.* People are going to continue to disappoint, irritate, and annoy you, especially if you allow this to happen. The question becomes, How are you going to deal with the stress associated with these conflicts? If you are going to last very long in this profession, you must develop ways to let things go. This means developing a lifestyle that

is balanced and healthy. Eat right. Sleep well. Get regular exercise. Avoid addictions. Find as much love as you can. Play and laugh. Do all those things that you think are good for your students to do.

9. *Diversify interests and commitments.* Teaching is only one part of who you are. Make sure that your life is filled with other interests and exciting things so that when school isn't going well or when you have a bad day, there are other things you can do to find satisfaction. Nothing contributes to vulnerability more than having all your self-esteem connected to one, and only one, endeavor.

10. *Don't work excessively at home.* By work, I don't mean only grading papers and doing schoolwork, but also just thinking about people who drive you crazy. Banish them from your head! Don't allow people to live inside you without your permission.

11. *Stop caring about things you can't change.* Nothing will drive you crazy faster than focusing on things you can't do anything about. That is what leads to helplessness and even depression. There are many things you cannot change (budget, administration, poverty, etc.) no matter what you do or how hard you try.

12. *Be selective about who you hang out with.* Your attitude, values, and morale are affected strongly by those you associate with most. If you hang around with people who complain, whine, and have negative attitudes, such an atmosphere will be contagious. Whenever possible, spend time with colleagues who are excited and enthusiastic about their work, as well as those who will challenge you when you start complaining too much about those who are driving you crazy.

Even when you cannot control other people or dictate that they abide by your rules, or when you find yourself unable to live up to their demands, you can assuredly function in such a way that you do not place yourself in such a vulnerable position. In order to work such conflicts through, there are several ways that you may wish to reorient your perspective on these relationships:

1. Think in terms of interactive effects and mutual responsibility rather than who did what to whom and who is the biggest villain.

2. Stop thinking in terms of winning and losing, but rather adopt an attitude that assumes both of you can get part of what you want.

3. Refuse to engage in or tolerate verbal abuse or disrespectful behavior.

4. Establish and enforce firm but reasonable limits during communication and emphasize respectful attention, responsive listening, and compromise.

5. Use a number of tactics and strategies that combine positions of power (assertiveness, threat, coercion, confrontation) and concession (compromise, compliance, empathy).

6. Remain flexible in your thinking and in your actions so that you are in a position to settle a conflict in a maximum number of different ways.

7. Remain committed to the notion that you can get much of what you want without antagonizing your adversary in such a way that continued conflict is likely.

## Conflict Resolution

One sure way to reduce problems in your classroom—with particular students or any disruption—is to teach appropriate ways of resolving conflicts. There are many such disputes that arise every day, every hour, with students fighting over everything from an accidental bump in the hallway to a full-fledged gang war. With alarming frequency, students are resorting to the use of lethal weapons to settle disputes, maiming and killing others who are believed to be at fault.

The subject of conflict plays a huge role in almost any content area. History, of course, is actually a discipline of conflict in which the story of humankind is reviewed in terms of war, skirmishes, intellectual debate, and fights over territory and expansion. Most good literature needs some sort of conflict and tension in order to work well. And of course, put more than two people in a room together for very long, and eventually, some conflict will arise.

It could be suggested that conflict is not only inevitable but natural. Most often, such disputes are "tribal" in origin, such that members of one particular group/sect/tribe/gang attempt to control limited resources, accumulate or protect territory, or otherwise exert their will over those in a more vulnerable position.

> Assyrians versus Babylonians, Romans versus Carthaginians, Moors versus Spaniards, Boers versus the English, Iroquois versus Algonquins, Paiutes versus Utes, Croats versus Serbs, Turks versus Armenians, Japanese versus Koreans, Peruvians versus Ecuadorians, Hutu versus Tutsi, Khmer Rouge versus Cambodians, Irish Catholics versus Protestants, Union versus the Confederacy, Bloods versus Crips, Arabs versus Jews, Romans versus Christians, Montagues versus Capulets, and Hatfields versus McCoys. The list goes on and on. (Kottler, 1997, p. 26)

Clearly, there is a long history of people fighting with one another. Such disputes are not only going to continue, but you'll only drive yourself more crazy if you think you can do something to stop disagreements altogether. In fact, the very process of conflict can be very helpful to people, as well as advancing knowledge, if conflicts are handled in ways that are respectful and follow some basic rules of discourse.

## Models of Resolution

You can prevent many problems in the future if you teach students (and yourself) how to settle conflicts in the most appropriate and effective way possible. Many such models exist that not only can be mastered in a relatively short time but also can be taught systematically to students. Osier and Fox (2001) suggest the following method for settling conflicts between elementary-age children:

1. *What's the problem?* The authors ask the identified "victims" of a dispute to talk about, or better yet, to write down what

was said or done to them that they didn't like. They are encouraged to detail what they felt during the experience and then what they did afterward.

2. *Exchange of perspectives.* In the second step, the two injured parties read one another's papers aloud. Participants are not allowed to debate or argue, they simply listen to one another's point of view. The emphasis throughout this process is not on winning or deciding who is right but only on solving the problem between them.

3. *What do I need to solve the problem?* In the next paper or worksheet, each combatant writes down what he or she wants to happen in order to feel better. What is it that is needed in order to solve the problem?

4. *Exchange of ideas.* Again, students read one another's view of things. If something is not understood, questions are allowed. At this point, however, it is *very* important that you control the dialogue so that things remain civil and focused only on solving the problem.

5. *Consensus seeking.* In this final and most difficult part, students circle the ideas on the other person's paper that they also believe could solve the problem. In other words, at this point the combatants are searching for areas of agreement.

With very young children, this process can be done by having them draw the problem. With older students, the same ideas can be adapted to their level of comprehension. The main idea is to teach ways to resolve disputes without resorting to hurtful interactions. This happens far more often under the following conditions:

- When people stop blaming others, or one another, for their problems
- When people don't overblame themselves, or take on too much responsibility, for what goes wrong
- When hurt and resentful feelings are expressed sensitively and appropriately
- When people hear and respond to one another
- When emotions like anger remain under control
- When the underlying causes of repeated conflicts are addressed

- When people commit themselves to act differently, and do so in front of witnesses
- When the focus of negotiation remains on the problem and how it can be resolved
- When each party is willing to compromise (to give up something) for mutual benefit.

Students (and most others) don't know how to resolve conflicts effectively. They tend to do the same things they see at home, in their neighborhoods, and on television—they resort to screaming, verbal abuse, fighting, and intimidation. They may not try more socially appropriate avenues because those are not within their repertoire. It is up to you to teach these skills, and just as important, to model them in the ways you address your own conflicts with others.

## Peer Mediation

Even better than having you be the one to settle disputes is allowing the students to take responsibility for this process. In peer mediation programs, volunteer students are trained to handle disputes between their agemates. This has a number of advantages, the most obvious of which are that there isn't the usual resentment toward authority and that children learn to take responsibility for settling their own disputes with minimal adult intervention.

In one model, Gilhooley and Scheuch (2000) present a structured program for training peer mediators that teaches them such things as establishing ground rules and understanding conflict as well as how to do active listening, problem solving, and negotiation. Role-playing situations are used to help kids practice their new skills in relatively controlled situations before they try them out in progressively more serious altercations.

It is necessary for you to implement a whole program in your school in order to introduce the basic principles to students in conflict. The main idea is that discussions will be respectful and guided toward cooperative problem solving to mutual satisfaction. Obviously, in order for this to operate effectively, all parties have to be reasonably motivated to work things through. As we have seen previously, some children enjoy tremendously the power that comes with stirring things up; they don't really want to resolve problems. That means you have to figure out ways to make sure they no longer "enjoy" the benefits associated with being a troublemaker.

Another role you can play in dispute resolution, whether as part of peer or teacher mediation, is to ensure that the atmosphere remains calm and objective. Some other things you can do yourself or teach students to do for themselves follow:

- Try to introduce fresh ways of looking at the problems, demonstrating as much flexibility as possible.
- Help participants to hear one another and to respond respectfully.
- Clarify the underlying issues at stake, the ones that may be represented by the present skirmish.
- Suggest resources that might be useful to the parties in finding some common ground.

## In Summary

I wish to close our discussion of working with challenging people by reviewing and reframing a few principles we have discussed. First of all, in many ways challenging people make your life interesting. They are inventive, creative, and passionate, and they feel very strongly about their beliefs, which may differ from your own. They stretch you in new ways and teach you about aspects of yourself (and the world) that you could not learn any other way.

Second, students who drive you crazy help you to look at your own need for control. Many of us became teachers in the first place because we like being the one in charge. We do not take kindly to others—especially people smaller than us—trying to challenge our authority. By definition, someone who is getting under your skin is making you feel powerless and helpless. You change this power balance not so much by altering their behavior as by changing your perception of the situation.

Last, remember that students whom you find difficult are not necessarily being resistant; they are simply cooperating in ways that are different from what you expect.

# References and Suggested Readings

Amatea, E. S. (1989). *Brief strategic interventions for school behavior problems.* San Francisco: Jossey-Bass.

Ayres, B. J., & Hedeen, D. L. (1998). Creating positive behavior support plans for students with significant behavioral challenges. *Rural Special Education Quarterly, 17*(3), 27-35.

Beck, A., & Freeman, A. (1990). *Cognitive therapy of personality disorders.* New York: Guilford.

Bemak, F., & Keys, S. (2000). *Violent and aggressive youth.* Thousand Oaks, CA: Corwin.

Blau, S., & Ellis, A. (Eds.). (1998). *Albert Ellis reader: Guide to well-being using Rational Emotive Behavior Therapy.* New York: Citadel.

Bonnington, S. B. (1993). Solution-focused brief therapy: Helpful interventions for school counselors. *The School Counselor, 41,* 126-128.

Bruce, M. A. (1995). Brief counseling: An effective model for change. *The School Counselor, 42,* 353-363.

Burden, P. R. (2000). *Powerful classroom management strategies.* Thousand Oaks, CA: Corwin.

Cade, B., & O'Hanlon, W. H. (1994). *A brief guide to brief therapy.* New York: Norton.

Campbell, C. A. (1991). Group guidance for academically under-motivated children. *Elementary School Guidance and Counseling, 25,* 302-307.

Canter, L., & Canter, M. (1993). *Succeeding with difficult students.* Santa Monica, CA: Canter and Associates.

Capuzzi, D. (1998). Adolescent suicide: Prevention and intervention. In J. Carlson & J. Lewis (Eds.), *Counseling the adolescent* (pp. 97-110). Denver, CO: Love.

Carns, A. W., & Carns, M. R. (1994). Making behavioral contracts successful. *The School Counselor, 42,* 155-160.

Davis-Johnson, S. P. (2001). *7 essentials for character discipline.* Thousand Oaks, CA: Corwin.

de Shazer, S. (1991). *Putting differences to work.* New York: Norton.

Delpit, L. (1995). *Other people's children: Cultural conflict in the classroom.* New York: New Press.

DiGiulio, R. (2000). *Positive classroom management* (2nd ed.). Thousand Oaks, CA: Corwin.

Downing, J., & Downing, S. (1991). Consultation with resistant parents. *Elementary School Guidance and Counseling, 25,* 296-301.

Downing, J., & Harrison, T. C. (1990). Dropout prevention: A practical approach. *The School Counselor, 38,* 67-74.

Ellis, A. (1996). *Better, deeper, and more enduring brief therapy.* New York: Brunner/Mazel.

Ellis, J., Hart, S., & Small-McGinley, J. (1998). The perspectives of difficult students on belonging and inclusion in the classroom. *Reclaiming Children and Youth, 7,* 142-146.

Evans, D. R., Hearn, M. T., Uhlemann, M., & Ivey, A. E. (2000). *Essential interviewing: A programmed approach to effective communication* (5th ed.). Pacific Grove, CA: Brooks/Cole.

Flick, G. L. (1999). *Managing difficult behavior in the classroom: A pocket guide for teachers.* Biloxi, MS: Seacoast.

Gilhooley, J., & Scheuch, N. S. (2000). *Using peer mediation in classrooms and schools.* Thousand Oaks, CA: Corwin.

Gill, V. (1998). *The ten commandments of good teaching.* Thousand Oaks, CA: Corwin.

Gootman, M. E. (2001). *The caring teacher's guide to discipline* (2nd ed.). Thousand Oaks, CA: Corwin.

Greenspan, S. I. (1995). *The challenging child*. Cambridge, MA: Perseus.

Hazler, R. J. (1998). *Helping in the hallways*. Thousand Oaks, CA: Corwin.

Hazler, R. J., Hoover, J., & Oliver, R. (1993). What do kids say about bullying? *Education Digest, 58*(7), 16-20.

Horne, A., & Campbell, L. F. (1998). Round pegs in square holes. In H. Forester-Miller & J. A. Kottler (Eds.), *Issues and challenges for group practitioners* (pp. 57-80). Denver, CO: Love.

Hunter, M. (1990). *Discipline that develops self-discipline*. Thousand Oaks, CA: Corwin.

Iwaniec, D., & Herbert, M. (1999). Multidimensional approach to helping emotionally abused and neglected children and abusive parents. *Children and Society, 13,* 365-379.

Johns, B. H., & Carr, V. G. (1995). *Techniques for managing verbally and physically aggressive students*. Denver, CO: Love.

Johnson, D. W. (2000). *Reaching out: Interpersonal effectiveness and self-actualization* (7th ed.). Boston: Allyn & Bacon.

King, A. (2001). *Demystifying the counseling process*. Boston: Allyn & Bacon.

Koenig, L. (2000). *Smart discipline for the classroom* (3rd ed.). Thousand Oaks, CA: Corwin.

Koplewicz, H. S. (1996). *It's nobody's fault: New hope and help for difficult children*. New York: Times Books.

Kottler, E., & Kottler, J. A. (2002). *Children with limited English: Teaching strategies for the regular classroom*. Thousand Oaks, CA: Corwin.

Kottler, J. A. (1992). *Compassionate therapy: Working with difficult clients*. San Francisco: Jossey-Bass.

Kottler, J. A. (1994). *Beyond blame: A new way of resolving conflicts in relationships*. San Francisco: Jossey-Bass.

Kottler, J. A. (1997). *What's really said in the teachers' lounge*. Thousand Oaks, CA: Corwin.

Kottler, J. A. (2000). *Nuts and bolts of helping*. Boston: Allyn & Bacon.

Kottler, J. A., & Kottler, E. (2000). *Counseling for teachers*. Thousand Oaks, CA: Corwin.

Kottler, J. A., Sexton, T., & Whiston, S. (1994). *The heart of healing: Relationships in therapy.* San Francisco: Jossey-Bass.

Kounin, J. S. (1970). *Discipline and group management in classrooms.* New York: Holt, Rinehart & Winston.

Kounin, J. S., Friesen, W. V., & Norton, A. E. (1966). Managing emotionally disturbed children in regular classrooms. *Journal of Educational Psychology, 57*(1), 1-13.

Lewis, A. (1992). Student motivation and learning: The role of the school counselor. *The School Counselor, 39,* 333-337.

Littrell, J. M., Malia, J. A., & Vanderwood, M. (1995). Single-session brief counseling in a high school. *Journal of Counseling and Development, 73,* 451-458.

Long, N. (1992). Managing a shooting incident. *Journal of Emotional and Behavioral Problems, 1*(1), 23-26.

Maag, J. W., & Forness, S. R. (1998). Depression in children and adolescents: Identification, assessment, and treatment. In J. Carlson & J. Lewis (Eds.), *Counseling the adolescent* (pp. 65-96). Denver, CO: Love.

Maas, P. (1997). *Underboss: Sammy the Bull Gravano's story of life in the Mafia.* New York: HarperCollins.

MacGrath, M. (1998). *The art of teaching peacefully.* London: David Fulton.

Madanes, C. (1981). *Strategic family therapy.* San Francisco: Jossey-Bass.

Marlowe, M. (1999). Reaching reluctant students. *Reclaiming Children and Youth, 7,* 242-245.

McEwan, E. K., & Damer, M. (2000). *Managing unmanageable students.* Thousand Oaks, CA: Corwin.

McMullin, R. E. (1999). *The new handbook of cognitive therapy techniques.* New York: Norton.

Metropolitan Life Insurance. (1986). *The Metropolitan Life Insurance survey of former teachers in America.* New York: Author.

Molnar, A., & Lindquist, B. (1990). *Changing problem behavior in the schools.* San Francisco: Jossey-Bass.

Montgomery, M. J. (1999). *Building bridges with parents.* Thousand Oaks, CA: Corwin.

Murphy, J. J. (1994). Working with what works: A solution-focused approach to school behavior problems. *The School Counselor, 42,* 59-65.

Nardone, G., & Watzlawick, P. (2001). *Brief strategic therapy.* Northvale, NJ: Jason Aronson.

National Center for Education Statistics. (1998). *Violence and discipline problems in U.S. public schools* (NCES 98-030). Washington, DC: Government Printing Office.

Neenan, M., & Dryden, W. (1999). *Rational Emotive Behaviour Therapy: Advances in theory and practice.* London: Whurr.

O'Hanlon, W. H. (2000). *Do one thing different.* New York: Quill.

Orange, C. (2000). *25 biggest mistakes teachers make and how to avoid them.* Thousand Oaks, CA: Corwin.

Osier, J. L., & Fox, H. P. (2001). *Settle conflicts right now!* Thousand Oaks, CA: Corwin.

Peeks, B. (1992). Protection and social context: Understanding a child's problem behavior. *Elementary School Guidance and Counseling, 26,* 295-304.

Philips, G., & Watts, T. (2001). *Rapid cognitive therapy.* New York: Crown.

Quick, E. K. (1996). *Doing what works in brief therapy.* San Diego, CA: Academic Press.

Ritchie, M. (1994). Counseling difficult children. *Canadian Journal of Counseling, 28,* 58-68.

Rosen, L. (1997). *School discipline: Best practices for administrators.* Thousand Oaks, CA: Corwin.

Roth, H. J. (1991). School counseling groups for violent and assaultive youth: The Willie M.'s. *Journal of Offender Rehabilitation, 16,* 113-131.

Seligman, L., & Gaaserud, L. (1994). Difficult clients: Who are they and how do we help them? *Canadian Journal of Counseling, 28,* 25-42.

Sells, S. P., Schiff, N., & Haley, J. (1998). *Treating the tough adolescent.* New York: Guilford.

Shields, J. D., & Green, R. J. (1996). POETICS: A systems approach to solving behavior problems in the classroom. *Elementary School Guidance and Counseling, 30,* 181-194.

Sklare, G. B. (1997). *Brief counseling that works: A solution-focused approach for school counselors.* Thousand Oaks, CA: Corwin.

Skramstad, T. (1998, Summer). Reaching resistant youth through writing. *Reaching Today's Youth,* 20-24.

Taffel, R. (2001). *Getting through to difficult kids and parents.* New York: Guilford.

Taylor, H. E., & Larson, S. (1998, March/April). Using cooperative learning with students who have attention deficit hyperactivity disorder. *Social Studies and the Young Learner,* 1-4.

Webb, W. (1992). Empowering at-risk children. *Elementary School Guidance and Counseling, 27,* 96-103.

Wessler, R., Hankin, S., & Stern, J. (2001). *Succeeding with difficult clients: Application of cognitive appraisal therapy.* New York: Academic Press.

Willison, B. G., & Masson, R. L. (1990). Therapeutic reparenting for the developmentally deprived student. *The School Counselor, 38,* 143-152.

Winslade, J., & Monk, G. (2000). *Narrative mediation: A new approach to conflict resolution.* San Francisco: Jossey-Bass.

Young, M. (2001). *Learning the art of helping: Building blocks and techniques.* Upper Saddle River, NJ: Merrill.

# Index

Addictions, students with, viii
  substance abuse, 15-16
Aggressive behavior, possible meanings
  of, 19. *See also* Aggressive
  students
Aggressive students, 16-23
  as contagious, 19-20
  as lesson material, 22-23
  classroom environment effects, 19
  dealing with, 20-22
  physically, 17-18
  protecting self from, 21
  protecting students from, 21
  questions to ask about, 24-25
  reacting to, 23
  verbally, 17, 18
  *See also* Violence, school; Violent
    students
Anxiety:
  students with chronic, 35
  classroom, 19
  *See also* Panic disorder, students with
Assault victims, students as, 17
At-risk students, 16
Attention deficit disorder, students with,
  15, 35
Attention-seeking students, viii
Autistic students, 35
Ayres, B. J., 67, 69

Beck, A., 82
Behavior:
  functional value, 27, 28
  protective role, 27
  *See also* Challenging students' behav-
    ior; Students' behavior, changing
Behavior support plan, 67-68
  example, 69
Belongingness, problems of, 71
Bemak, F., 20
Blau, S., 82
Bored students, viii
Brief therapy, 77
  assumptions, 77-79
Bullying, 17, 21
  victims, 17, 19
Burden, P. R., 103
Burnout, teacher, 87

Cade, B., 77
Campbell, C. A., 82
Canter, L., 101, 102
Canter, M., 101, 102
Capuzzi, D., 14
Carr, V. G., 20
Challenging students:
  chronic, 40
  creating, 35-37, 52
  engaging, 51-52
  home life, 30
  needs, 102
  protecting self from, 42-44
  reactions to, 7
  reasons for, 38

varied opinions about, 4-6
*See also specific types of students*;
    Challenging students' behavior
Challenging students' behavior, 1-2,
    40-41, 102, 104
    attention-loving and, 30-31
    disasters and, 30
    feelings of empowerment and, 29-30
    maintaining status quo and, 31-32
    organizational disputes and, 30
    reasons for, 104
    responsibility avoidance and, 31
    secondary gains, 29-32
    understanding, 26-38
    *See also* Conflict; Family, student
        behavior and
Codependence:
    versus empathy, 57
Cognitive therapy, 82
    teachers' self-use, 83-85
Colleagues, difficult, 86-87
    abuse from, 97-99
    administrators, 89
    dealing with abuse from, 98-99
    who don't understand, 87-89
    *See also* Conflict
Conflict:
    competition for opportunities/
        resources, 88
    control issues and, 34
    distance maintenance and, 33-34
    functions of, 32-35
    ideological arguments, 88
    personality clashes, 88
    reasons for organizational, 88
    release of tension and, 33
    reorienting relationships and, 108
    taking personally, 53-54
    underlying unresolved issues and,
        34-35
    *See also* Challenging students'
        behavior; Conflict resolution,
        teaching; Conflict resolution
        models; Conflicts, resolving
        teacher-student
Conflict resolution, teaching, 108-112

history content area, 108-109
Conflict resolution models, 109-111
    elementary-age children, 109-110
    secondary-age children, 110-111
    *See also* Peer mediation
Conflicts, resolving teacher-student,
    82-85
    challenge thinking, 82-83
    teachers' self-use of cognitive
        approaches, 83-85
Consequences, 103
    versus punishment, 103
Cultural background, challenging
    students and, 3

Damer, M., 40
Demoralization, teacher, 87
Depressed students, 35, 57
    school-age, 13-14
    *See also* Depression
Depression:
    bullying and, 17
    interventions, 14
    referral, 13
    *See also* Depressed students;
        Non-communicative students;
        Suicide; Withdrawn students
de Shazer, S., 77, 92
DiGiulio, R., 35
Disobedience:
    as creative cooperation, 62-63
Disrespectful students, viii, 4, 18
Disruptive students, viii, 1
Dryden, W., 82

Ellis, A., 82
Ellis, J., 71
Enuresis, students and, 35
Evans, D. R., 73
Explosive personality/temperament,
    aggressive/violent behavior and, 19

Failure:
    advantages, 48-51
    change stimulus, 49
    encouraging flexibility, 49-50

improving frustration tolerance, 50
promoting reflection, 48-49
providing useful information, 51
teachers' fear of, 44
teaching humility, 50-51
Family, student behavior and:
    discipline and, 30
    marital conflict and, 30
    transitions and, 30
    hierarchical disorders and, 30
    *See also* Parents, challenging
        students'
Forness, S. R., 13
Fox, H. P., 109
Freeman, A., 82
Freud, Sigmund, 42
Friesen, W. V., 100

Gilhooley, J., 111
Gootman, M. E., 10, 103, 104
Gravano, Sammy "The Bull," 18-19

Haley, J., 77
Hankin, S., 82
Hart, S., 71
Hazler, R. J., 17
Hearn, M. T., 73
Hedeen, D. L., 67, 69
Herbert, M., 92
Hidden agenda, students with, 12
Hoover, J., 17
Hostile students, viii, 10

Impulse disorder, aggressive/violent
        behavior and, 19
Ivey, A. E., 73
Iwaniec, D., 92

Johns, B. H., 20
Johnson, D. W., 73

Keys, S., 20
King, A., 73
Koplewicz, H. S., 35
Kottler, E., 13, 72
Kottler, J. A., 13, 35, 72, 72, 73, 109

Kounin, J. S., 100

Larson, S., 71
Learning disorders, students with, 18
    aggressive/violent behavior and, 19
    dyslexia, 18-19
Lewis, A., 83
Littrell, J. M., 77
Long, N., 17

Maag, J. W., 13
Maas, P., 19
MacGrath, M., 21, 67
Madanes, C., 92
Malia, J. A., 77
Manipulative students, viii, 12
    aggressive/violent behavior and, 19
Mantras, 57-58
    samples, 58
Marlowe, M., 68
Masson, R. L., 67
McEwan, E. K., 40
McMullin, R. E., 82
Mentally ill students, 15
Mind-game-playing students, 1, 12
Miracle question technique, 79-80
Modeling behavior, home and:
    aggressive/violent behavior and, 19

Nardone, G., 77
National Center for Education Statistics,
        17
Neenan, M., 82
Non-communicative students, 12-15
    culture and, 12-13
    depression and, 13
    limited English proficiency and, 13
    low self-esteem and, 13
Norton, A. E., 100
Obsessive-compulsive disorder, students
        with, 35
O'Hanlon, W. H., 77, 92
Oliver, R., 17
Osier, J. L., 109

Panic disorder, students with, 35

Parents, challenging students':
    categories, 90
    fighting teachers, 89-92
    part of problem, 30
    recruiting assistance from, 90
    strategies, 93-94
    winning support from, 90
    *See also* Family, student behavior and
Parent-teacher conferences, 28-29
    basic rules, 76
Peeks, B., 28
Peer group normative behavior,
        aggressive/violent behavior and,
        19
Peer mediation, 111-112
    advantages, 111
    maintaining calm atmosphere, 112
Personality disorders, students with, 52
Philips, G., 82
Physiologically impaired students, 15-16,
        35. *See also* Addictions, students
        with; Attention deficit disorder,
        students with; Mentally ill students
Power, aggressive/violent behavior and,
        19
Prevention, problem, 100-101
    attention to feedback, 103-105
    maintaining momentum. 105-108
    *See also* Proactive intervention
Proactive intervention, 102
    specific types, 104
    strategies, 101-103
    versus reactive intervention, 102
    *See also* Consequences
Problem-solving strategy, learned:
    aggressive/violent behavior and, 19
Problem-solving therapists, 79. *See also*
        Miracle question technique
Punishment, 103
    versus consequences, 103

Quick, E. K., 92

Reactive intervention:
    "discipline with capital D," 103
    "low-key discipline," 103

    *See also* Punishment
Resistant students, 41-42, 47-48
    dealing effectively with, 42
Respect, demand for:
    aggressive/violent behavior and, 19
Retribution/revenge, aggressive/violent
        behavior and, 19
Roth, H. J., 11
Rule-violating students, 9-10
    boundaries and, 10
    reasons, 9-10

Scheuch, N. S., 111
Schiff, N., 77
Schizophrenic students, 35
School shootings, 17
Self-talk, 57-58, 85
    students' negative, 82
Sells, S. P., 77
Sklare, G. B., 77
Skramstad, T., 71
Small-McGinley, J., 71
Social phobia, bullying and, 17
Staff lounge talk, 3, 54-55, 61
Stern, J., 82
Strategic interventions, teacher, 77-81
Strategic therapists, 77
Strategic therapy, 77
    rules, 92-93
Stress disorders, teacher, 87
Students' behavior, rules for changing,
        66-77
    active listening, 72
    communication improvement, 71-72
    conferences, 75-76
    counseling, 72-73
    duration, 81
    intensity, 81
    location, 81
    needy student, 67
    partner, 73-75
    primacy of relationship, 68-71
    rate, 81
    sequence, 81
    shaking things up, 81
    *See also* Behavior support plan

Suicide:
  attempts, 17
  myth versus reality, 14
  risk factors, 14-15

Taffel, R., 75, 76
Taylor, H. E., 71
Teachers, challenging students and, 36-37
  approval issues, 47
  bad communication, 36
  countertransference, 46, 52
  demanding expectations, 51
  detachment, 43
  evaluation of situation, 45
  fear of failure, 44
  helping self, 52-53
  helplessness feelings, 44
  incompetence feelings, 44, 47
  intimacy issues, 47
  invalid assumptions, 36
  missing information, 36
  need for control, 44
  painful childhood memories, 44
  personal issues, 46-47, 51
  power issues, 47
  strategies for maintaining momentum, 105-108
  unmet needs, 52
  See also Challenging students
Teachers, professional dropout of, 87
Teachers' behavior:
  accepting self limits, 106
  attending to relationships, 106
  being flexible, 63-65
  changing, 53, 95-96
  detachment, 56-57
  diversifying interests, 107
  finding best in people, 106
  focusing on right, 80-81
  having realistic expectations, 105
  keeping sense of humor, 62, 106
  letting go, 76-77, 107
  limiting at-home work, 107

metabolizing stress, 106-107
  processing disappointments internally, 59-61
  reframing problems, 62-63
  selecting friends wisely, 107
  self-help first, 65
  self-talk, 57-58
  stop complaining, 61-62
  taking risks, 105-106
  taking victories, 106
Tourette's syndrome, students with, 35
Troubled students, symptoms of, 17

Uhlemann, M., 73
Unmotivated students, viii, 11-12

Vanderwood, M., 77
Violence, school:
  assaults with deadly weapons, 17
  fights, 17
  media violence and, 18
  rape, 17
  See also Bullying; School shootings; Violent students
Violent behavior, possible meanings of, 19
Violent students, viii, 10-11, 17. See also Aggressive students; Learning disorders, students with; School shootings; Violence, school

Watts, T., 82
Watzlawick, P., 77
Webb, W., 16
Wessler, R., 82
Willison, B. G., 67
Withdrawn students, viii, 1, 11, 12, 13, 57
  bullying and, 17
  depression and, 13
"Working the system," students, 12

Young, M., 73

## CORWIN
## PRESS

The Corwin Press logo—a raven striding across an open book—represents the happy union of courage and learning. We are a professional-level publisher of books and journals for K-12 educators, and we are committed to creating and providing resources that embody these qualities. Corwin's motto is "Success for All Learners."